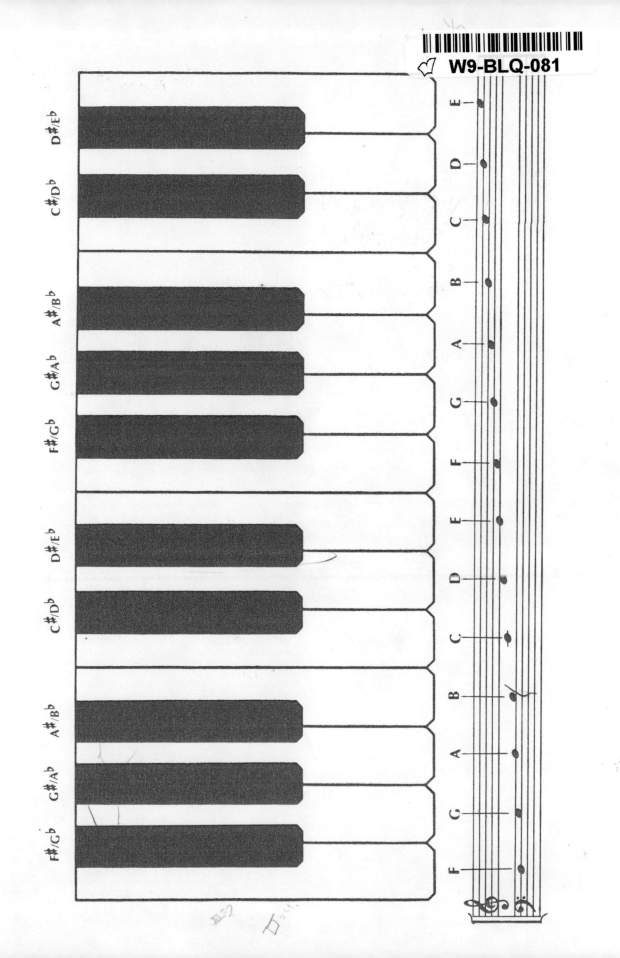

Silver Burdett

music
Centennial Edition

Elizabeth Crook

Bennett Reimer

David S. Walker

SILVER BURDETT COMPANY MORRISTOWN, NEW JERSEY

ATLANTA, GA · CINCINNATI, OH · DALLAS, TX · NORTHFIELD, IL · SAN CARLOS, CA · AGINCOURT, ONTARIO

Contents

Using What You Know About Rhythm

Sounds give us a feeling of movement. The movement of sounds in music is called *rhythm*. This section will explore many of the ways that rhythm works in music.

Paintings can also give us a feeling of movement, even though nothing is actually moving.

Which of the paintings below gives more feeling of stillness?
Which gives more feeling of movement?
Why?

MIRO: DOG BARKING AT THE MOON

MIRO: CARNIVAL OF HARLEQUIN

Poems have movement also. How is fast and slow movement created in this poem?

SWIFT THINGS ARE BEAUTIFUL

Swift things are beautiful:
Swallows and deer,
And lightning that falls
Bright-veined and clear,
Rivers and meteors,
Wind in the wheat,
The strong-withered horse,
The runner's sure feet.

And slow things are beautiful:
The closing of day,
The pause of the wave
That curves downward to spray,
The ember that crumbles,
The opening flower,
And the ox that moves on
In the quiet of power.

Elizabeth J. Coatsworth

What are the swift things mentioned in the first stanza? What are the slow things mentioned in the second stanza? As you read the poem again, feel the fast or slow movement of what your mind "sees."

Artists and designers can give a feeling of movement by the way they make things look. How has the artist given a feeling of movement to this airplane?

CLAP-SNAP THE STEADY BEAT

Show the steady beat in this popular American folk song by doing a clap-snap pattern. Try this one with the recording. Then make up a pattern of your own.

clap   snap   clap   snap

Mama Don't 'Low

AMERICAN FOLK SONG

1.
2. Ma-ma don't 'low   no { gui - tar   play-in' round here,
3.   { ban - jo   pick-in' round here,
                             { rock song sing-in' round here,

Ma-ma don't 'low   no { gui - tar   play-in' round here,
                       { ban - jo   pick-in' round here,
                       { rock song sing-in' round here,

I don't care what Ma-ma don't 'low, Gon-na { play my gui - tar an - y - how,
                                            { pick my ban - jo an - y - how,
                                            { sing my rock songs an - y - how,

Ma-ma don't 'low   no { gui - tar   play-in' round here.
                       { ban - jo   pick-in' round here.
                       { rock song sing-in' round here.

📖 For recorder parts, see p. 207.

📖 For more practice feeling the steady beat, see p. 222.

PLAY THE STEADY BEAT

Play the steady beat on the Autoharp to accompany "Mama Don't 'Low." You will need the G, D_7, and C chords. The letter names above the music will tell you when to change from one chord to another.

Which pattern shows the steady beat? Try strumming one of the other rhythm patterns.

To accompany "Mama Don't 'Low" on a guitar, find the G and D strings. The photograph will help you. Follow the chord letters in the music and pluck the single string in one of the rhythm patterns shown above. Pluck the G string for the G and C chords; pluck the D string for the D_7 chord.

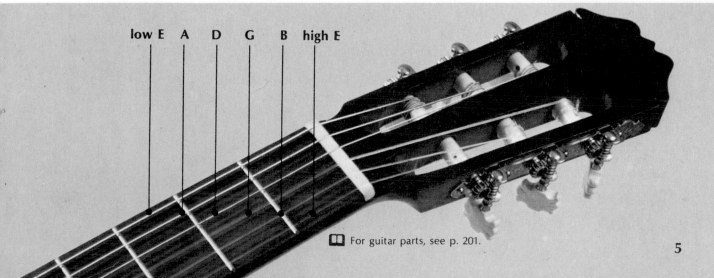

low E   A   D   G   B   high E

For guitar parts, see p. 201.

5

CHANGING TEMPO

Before playing the game, listen to the recording. Does the beat of this chant get faster or slower?

Sasa Akroma

SINGING GAME FROM AFRICA

FROM AFRICAN SONGS AND GAMES FOR CHILDREN COMPILED AND TRANSCRIBED BY KOJO FOSU BAIDEN AND GERALDINE SLAUGHTER. © 1970, KOJO FOSU BAIDEN AND GERALDINE SLAUGHTER.

Sah sah kroh mah woh nay ah woh chay chay nkoh koh mah.

Sah sah kroh mah woh nay ah woh chay chay nkoh koh mah.

AFRICAN BLOCK-PASSING GAME

Players sit in a circle. Each player holds a block of wood in the right hand. (Use only one hand throughout the game.)

On the strong beats (marked with an *X*), place your block in front of the player on your right. On the weak beats, pick up the block that has been placed in front of you.

Keep the blocks moving. When the *tempo* of the music gets faster, your movements will get faster. If you miss a beat, or drop or throw a block, you're out!

When you play the game, your two motions—pass and pick up—show the beats moving in twos—in a meter of 2. This is shown by the top number in the meter signature at the beginning of the song. For another block-passing game, see p. 239.

6

DANCE THE STEADY BEAT

Sandy Ree is a favorite dance in the West Indies. The basic step shows beats in 4. The dance is done with a sideways step and a "chug" on the fourth beat of each measure. (A "chug" is a hop backward without the foot leaving the floor.)

Sandy Ree may be danced alone or facing a partner.

Sandy Ree

SLAVE SONG FROM THE GEORGIA SEA ISLANDS

NEW WORDS & NEW MUSIC ADAPTATION BY BESSIE JONES & THE SEA ISLAND SINGERS. TRO—© COPYRIGHT 1972 LUDLOW MUSIC INC., NEW YORK, N.Y. USED BY PERMISSION.

Way down yon - der,____ San - dy Ree,____ Where I come from,

San - dy Ree,____ Girls____ love boys,____ San - dy Ree,____ like a

hog loves corn, San - dy Ree.____ Oh,____ babe,____

San - dy Ree,____ Oh,____ babe,____ San - dy Ree,____

Oh, babe,____ San - dy Ree,____ Oh,____ babe, San - dy Ree.____

2. Dog on the porch, . . .
   Kicking off fleas, . . .
   Chicken in the yard, . . .
   Scratching up peas, . . .

3. Your dog bark, . . .
   He don't see nothin', . . .
   My dog bark, . . .
   He done see somethin', . . .

For other movement activities, see pp. 237–250.

7

HAND JIVE IN 3

As you listen to the recording, keep the steady beat using a hand-jive motion to match the meter in 3.

clap | snap fingers R.H. | snap fingers L.H.

Shrimp Boats

WORDS AND MUSIC BY PAUL HOWARD AND PAUL WESTON

USED BY PERMISSION OF HANOVER MUSIC CORPORATION.

Shrimp boats is a-com-in', their sails are in sight.

Shrimp boats is a-com-in', there's danc-in' to-night.

Why don't you hur-ry, hur-ry, hur-ry home?

Why don't you hur-ry, hur-ry, hur-ry home?

Shrimp boats is a-com-in', there's danc-in' to-night.

Tap the rhythm made by the words in the first color box. Then find other phrases that have the same pattern.

Tap the rhythm made by the words in the second color box. Then find another phrase that has the same pattern.

Compare the two rhythm patterns you tapped.

A RHYTHM PATTERN THAT REPEATS

This song uses a rhythm pattern (shown in the color box) over and over.

Big Rock Candy Mountain

AMERICAN FOLK SONG

1. In the Big Rock Can - dy Moun-tain There's a land that's fair and bright,
2. In the Big Rock Can - dy Moun-tain All the cows have wood-en legs,

Where the hand-outs grow on bush - es, And you sleep out ev - 'ry night;
And the bull-dogs all are tooth-less, And the hens lay soft-boiled eggs,

Where the box - cars all are emp - ty, And the sun shines ev - 'ry day,
All the trees are full of ap - ples, And the barns are full of hay,

Oh, I'm bound to go where there is - n't an - y snow, Where the
There's a lake of stew and_____ so - da pop,_____ too, You can

rain does-n't fall and the wind does-n't blow, In the Big Rock Can - dy
paddle all a-round in a big ca - noe, In the Big Rock Can - dy

Moun - tain.
Moun - tain. Oh, the buzz-in' of the bees in the syc - a-more trees Round the

so - da wa - ter foun - tain, Where the lem - on - ade springs and the

blue - bird sings In the Big Rock Can - dy Moun - tain.

PATTERNS FOR TAMBOURINE

As you listen to this song, play the steady beat on a
tambourine. In what meter will you play? How do you know?

Toembaï ROUND FROM ISRAEL

USED BY PERMISSION OF WORLD AROUND SONGS.

I

Toem - baï, toem - baï, toem - baï, toem - baï, toem - baï, toem - baï, toem - baï.

II

Tra la la la la la la la la la la la la la.

III

Tra la la la la la la la la la la la la la la la la.

Each of the three rhythm patterns below is taken from the song.
Two of the patterns have accents. (An accent is a sudden
loudness.) How will you play an accent on a tambourine?
Choose a pattern to play throughout the song.

steady beat

10

DIVIDING THE STEADY BEAT

This song from Canada has two sections, A and B. Which one uses mostly eighth notes?

Vive la Canadienne!

FOLK SONG FROM CANADA   ENGLISH VERSION BY ROSEMARY JACQUES

1. Vi - ve la Ca - na - dien - ne! Vo - le, mon coeur,
1. Here's to the girl from Ca - na - da! How she makes my

vo - le! Vi - ve la Ca - na - dien - ne Et
poor___ heart___ beat! Here's to the girl from Ca - na - da With

ses jo - lis yeux doux, Et ses jo - lis yeux
eyes so___ ver - y sweet. Her pret - ty eyes are

doux, doux, doux, Et ses jo - lis yeux doux.___
ver - y sweet, Her eyes are ver - y sweet.___

2. On danse avec nos blondes,
   Vole, mon coeur, vole!
   On danse avec nos blondes;
   Nous changeons tour à tour,
   Nous changeons tour à tour, tour, tour,
   Nous changeons tour à tour.

2. *Someone is dancing with her now,*
   How she makes my poor heart beat!
   Someone is dancing with her now,
   But soon we two shall meet.
   But very soon we two shall meet,
   But soon we two shall meet.

The steady beat can be divided to make different rhythm patterns. Find these patterns in section A.

For guitar fingerings, see p. 204.

11

GROUPS OF 2 AND 3

Sometimes music from Greece uses a rhythm pattern combining groups of three and groups of two, making a meter of 7.

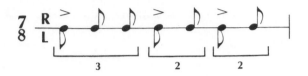

Practice this pattern on a drum to play with the recording. The first note of each set of threes and twos is accented. The pattern of accents creates its own rhythm. Take turns playing either part to accompany the singing.

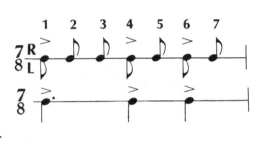

Samiotissa

MUSIC BY D. A. VERGONI   ENGLISH WORDS BY STELLA PHREDOPOLOUS

MELODY COPYRIGHT 1950 BY MICHAEL GAETANOS, ATHENS

Sa - mio - tis - sa, Sa - mio - tis - sa, You will re-turn to Sa -

mos._____ Sa - mio - tis - sa, Sa - mio - tis - sa, Is-land of beau-ty and de-

light._____ You will come home a - gain to me, Sa-mio-tis - sa, There's

mu - sic in the sum-mer night. _____ You will come home a - gain to

me, Sa-mio - tis - sa, There's mu - sic in the sum-mer night. _____

A CYCLE OF 7 BEATS

Rhythm pattern is used in music throughout the world. In India, a rhythm cycle, called a *tala*, decides the pattern.

The tala used to accompany this music has seven beats. Follow the circle of seven beats as you listen to the tala played on a drum.

Try clapping on the beats marked with an *X*.

🔘 Raga Yaman

📖 For more about tala, see p. 73.

📖 For more about the music of India, see Style: Music of India, pp. 166–168.

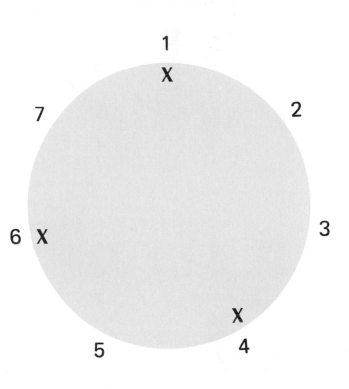

SOUND PIECE 1   A Tic-Tac-Toe in Rhythm   Wynn Check

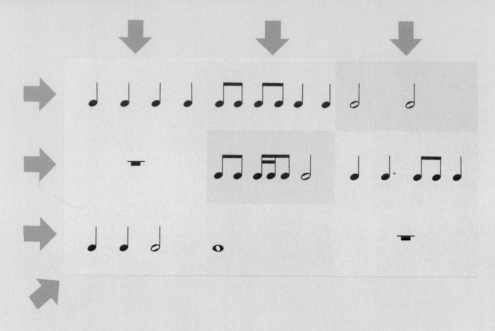

To play "A Tic-Tac-Toe in Rhythm," tap or clap the patterns in any three boxes, one after the other, by following the path of any arrow. For silence, feel the beat without tapping.

You can make the piece longer by following the path of more than one arrow. Plan ahead. Which arrows will you follow?

When you have your plan, experiment with these ideas.

• Add different tone colors by playing *Sound Piece 1* on a percussion instrument, a recorder, a guitar—or an instrument you invent.

• Set a tempo before you begin. Will it be very fast, fast, moderate, slow, or very slow?

• Choose a dynamic level for each part. Which part will be soft? Which will be loud? Which will be moderate?

Sound Piece 1 can be played by one person or by several people, starting together or at different times. All choose their own starting place.

After playing *Sound Piece 1,* compose your own sound piece. Use any arrangement of boxes, any rhythm patterns, and any instruments. Here is an example.

Teach others to play your sound piece by explaining the idea, playing it for them, or helping them figure it out from your notation.

CALL CHART 1: Rhythm 　　Treni: *Interlude*

This call chart will help you hear some of the ways rhythm works in music. When a number is called, find that number on the call chart. Next to the number will be the word or words that describe what you are hearing.

1	*STEADY BEAT—METER IN 2*	6	*STEADY BEAT—METER IN 3*
2	*CHANGE OF TEMPO*	7	*CHANGE OF TEMPO*
3	*STEADY BEAT*	8	*STEADY BEAT—METER IN 2*
4	*CHANGE OF TEMPO*	9	*CHANGE OF TEMPO*
5	*STEADY BEAT*	10	*STEADY BEAT*

On p. 18 you will find a list of qualities that "ears hear" when you listen to music.

Look at the list when you listen to this piece. It will help you hear what is going on in the music.

🎵 Ibert: *Entr'acte*

In *Entr'acte* you heard and experienced sounds for their own sake. No mind-pictures or stories or moods were needed—just music alone. Such music is called *absolute music.*

When a piece is based on a story, or when sounds suggest and describe a series of events, the music is called *program music.*

Symphonie fantastique describes the dreams of a young man in love. The part you will hear, the fourth movement, is a nightmare in which he is being led to his execution for killing his loved one, a beautiful actress. Each time she appears in his dreams, a haunting melody is played by the clarinet.

As you listen, choose as many words from p. 18 as you can to describe what you hear. Remember, in program music the story is just one part of all the musical things to hear.

🎵 Berlioz: *Symphonie fantastique,* "March to the Scaffold"

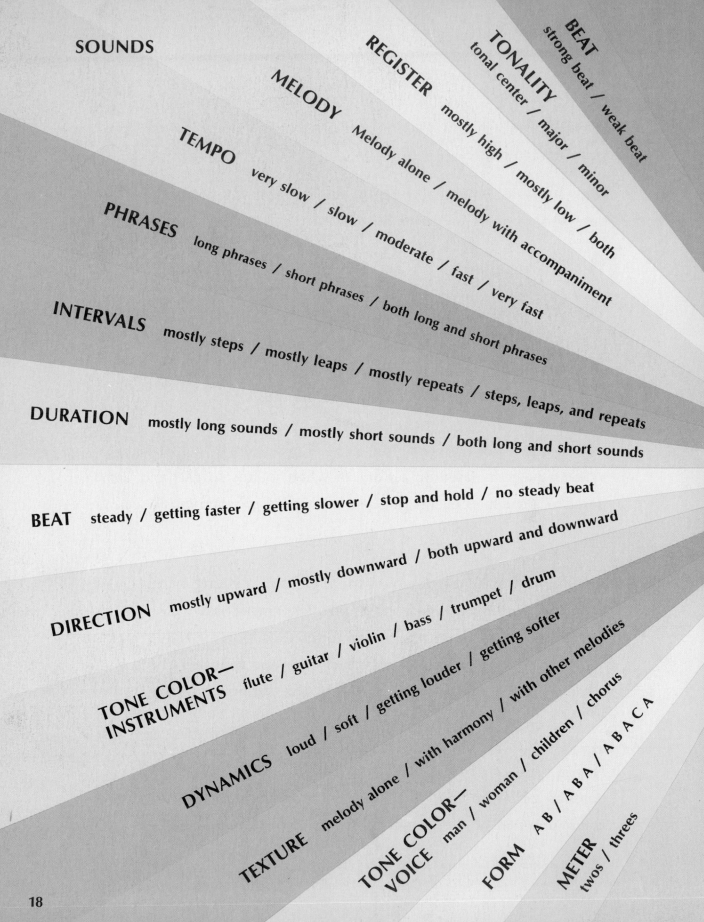

SOUNDS

BEAT strong beat / weak beat

TONALITY tonal center / major / minor

REGISTER mostly high / mostly low / both

MELODY Melody alone / melody with accompaniment

TEMPO very slow / slow / moderate / fast / very fast

PHRASES long phrases / short phrases / both long and short phrases

INTERVALS mostly steps / mostly leaps / mostly repeats / steps, leaps, and repeats

DURATION mostly long sounds / mostly short sounds / both long and short sounds

BEAT steady / getting faster / getting slower / stop and hold / no steady beat

DIRECTION mostly upward / mostly downward / both upward and downward

TONE COLOR— INSTRUMENTS flute / guitar / violin / bass / trumpet / drum

DYNAMICS loud / soft / getting louder / getting softer

TEXTURE melody alone / with harmony / with other melodies

TONE COLOR— VOICE man / woman / children / chorus

FORM A B / A B A / A B A C A

METER twos / threes

18

WHAT HAPPENS WHEN YOU LISTEN TO MUSIC?

MIND
perceives
It sorts out what the sounds
are doing and how they are
related to each other.

Ears
hear

FEELINGS
react
You become involved by
responding to what the
sounds are doing.

Sounds + Ears + Mind + Feelings = Listening Experience

19

More About Rhythm

CHANGING METER

What happens to the meter in this song? To find out, look at
the notation or listen to the recording.

Mineira de Minas

COMPOSER UNKNOWN   ENGLISH WORDS BY ROSEMARY JACQUES

I am a mi-nei-ra de Mi - nas, A mi-
nei - ra de Mi - nas Ge - rais. _____ And
you're a ca - rio - ca from Ri - o, From
Ri - o, that won-der-ful place. _____ Turn, turn, turn,
turn a-round and face the oth - er way, Clap your hands to-geth - er,
Turn a - round and face the oth - er way. Turn, turn, turn,
turn to fa - ther, turn to moth - er, Turn to one and then the oth - er,
Clap your hands to - geth - er, shout, "Hoo - ray!"

📖 For guitar fingerings, see p. 204.

📖 For percussion parts, see pp. 224 and 225.

A SONG IN THREE METERS

What is the meter plan in this song? To find out, clap or tap the beats as you listen to the recording.

Look Out!

WORDS AND MUSIC BY DORIS HAYS

© 1973 Doris Hays

Look out! Off the ground, turn a - round, what's that sound?

It's that rock - et roar - ing in the sky, just a speck in my eye,

Won - der if they're fly - ing to the moon, or to Mars, or Nep - tune,

Or some dis - tant star So ver - y far that we are like - ly to

run right out of breath!

A THREE-PART RHYTHM ROUND

Form a group with two friends and play the rhythm of the words in "Look Out!" on percussion instruments.

Using three different instruments will make the rhythm round more interesting.

📖 For percussion parts, see p. 226.

PATTERNS FOR TAMBOURINE

As you listen to the recording, play a tambourine on each beat
to accompany this folk song from Israel. This will help you feel
the change in tempo as the song is repeated.

Hallelujah FOLK SONG FROM ISRAEL

FROM GOOD TIMES SONG BOOK BY JAMES F. LEISY, PUBLISHED BY ABINGDON PRESS.

Hal - le - lu - jah, hal - le - lu - jah, hal - le - lu - jah, hal - le - lu!

Hal - le - lu - jah, hal - le - lu - jah, hal - le - lu - jah, hal - le - lu!

Hal - le - lu - jah, hal - le - lu, hal - le - lu - jah, hal - le - lu!

Hal - le - lu - jah, hal - le - lu - jah, hal - le - lu - jah, hal - le - lu!

When you can play the steady beat, try playing one of these
rhythm patterns throughout the song.

Notice that the beat shown by a quarter note (♩) can be
divided into two sounds (♫), called eighth notes.

22

WORD PATTERNS

In every language the rhythm of the words makes its own
patterns. Discover the patterns of long and short sounds made
by the Spanish words in this song in 3 meter.

El Capotín

FOLK SONG FROM PUERTO RICO

Try playing recorder or bells to accompany Section B. Improvise
(make up) your own rhythm pattern on the tone A.

A SYNCOPATED PATTERN

There are many ways to combine long and short sounds to create rhythm patterns. In this song you will hear a pattern that gives the music a special feeling called *syncopation*.

As you listen to the recording, clap the steady beat. This will help you feel the syncopated patterns when they come in the song.

I'm Gonna Sing Out

WORDS AND MUSIC BY DAVID EDDLEMAN

Down in_____ my feet I got a rhy - thm mov - in',

Feel - in'_____ the beat I got the mu - sic mov - in',

Deep in_____ my heart I hear a song a - sing - in',

Mov - in'_____ a - long in my soul.

Lord,_____ I'm gon - na sing out,_____ sing out, my

Lord,_____ I'm gon - na sing out,_____ sing out, yes,

Clap this syncopated rhythm pattern ♫♫♪ each time it comes in the song. How many times does it appear?

📖 For more about syncopation, see p. 234.

ADD A COUNTERMELODY

Try singing a harmony part for the B section of "I'm Gonna Sing Out." Does this countermelody use syncopation?

PATTERNS FOR PERCUSSION

Make up your own "bamboo walk." You will find some
suggestions for "fancy steps" on p. 238 in your book.

Thank You for the Chris'mus

FOLK SONG FROM JAMAICA

COLLECTED AND TRANSCRIBED BY OLIVE LEWIN   REPRINTED BY PERMISSION OF MISS OLIVE LEWIN AND THE ORGANIZATION OF AMERICAN STATES.

Thank you for ____ the Chris'-mus, Thank you for ____ the
New Year, And thank you for ____ the chance to live ____ to
see an-oth-er Chris'-mus La la la la, Do-in' the
            New Year
bam-boo walk, ____ La la la la, Do-in' the bam-boo walk. ____

Play one of these parts to accompany the singing and stepping.

Notice how quarter and eighth notes are used in $\frac{4}{4}$ meter.

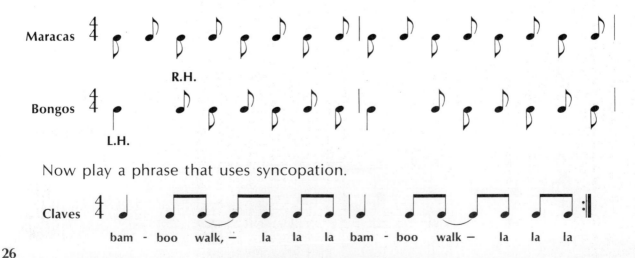

Now play a phrase that uses syncopation.

Claves

bam - boo walk, – la la la bam - boo walk – la la la

WORDS MAKE PATTERNS

Listen for the rhythm pattern made by the words of this song.

Do you hear long sounds, short sounds, or both?

Do you hear syncopation?

Pat-a-Pan

EARLY BURGUNDIAN FRENCH CAROL   ENGLISH WORDS BY ROSEMARY JACQUES

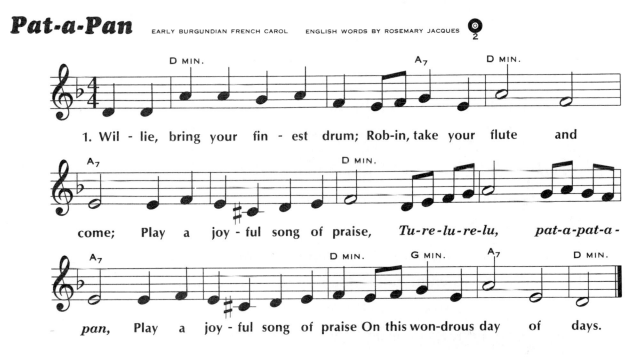

1. Wil - lie, bring your fin - est drum; Rob-in, take your flute and come; Play a joy - ful song of praise, *Tu-re-lu-re-lu,* pat-a-pat-a-*pan,* Play a joy - ful song of praise On this won-drous day of days.

2. Long ago on Christmas morn
   When the holy Child was born,
   Shepherds from the fields did come,
   Turelurelu, patapatapan,
   Shepherds from the fields did come
   Playing on their pipe and drum.

3. So 'tis fitting on this day
   That on instruments we play,
   Like the humble shepherd men,
   Turelurelu, patapatapan,
   Like the humble shepherd men
   Who were there in Bethlehem.

PAT-A-PAN ACCOMPANIMENTS

For other rhythm parts, see p. 227.

• Play the rhythm of the melody on a small drum.

• Play an added part on recorder or bells.

Recorder or Bells   **Play throughout**

Play throughout

27

Style: Music of Africa

A STORY IN SONG

The Shona people of Rhodesia tell the story about Karingano, a beautiful girl whose mother keeps her in a cave to protect her from young men. So that food can be brought to her, Karingano is told to come out of the cave only when she hears her mother singing.

The storyteller sings part of the story and the audience joins in singing *Mai Wakaringano,* which means "Mother of Karingano."

As you listen to the song, respond to the story just as the Shona people do, by singing the response.

🔘 *Mai Wakaringano*
2

If you were a young person growing up in Africa, you might learn music by listening rather than by reading notation. You might respond to stories like the story of Karingano, or you might make work less tiresome by learning to sing a song.

In this grinding song, two women are complaining about Debura's lazy husband while they grind grain between rocks to make flour. One woman sings the leader's part (call); the other sings the responses.

🔘 Debura
2

28

RATTLES AND DRUMS

Sometimes people in Shona society dance to the sounds of
rattles and various-sized drums. Listen for the rhythm pattern
played on the rattle throughout this dance music.

♫ Kalanga Dance

♩ ♩ ♪ ♩ ♩ ♩ ♪
1 2 3 4 5 6 7 8 9 10 11 12

When you listen again, hear the drums play different rhythms
above this basic pattern. One of the drums is being rubbed with
a stick. The others are struck.

AFRICAN INSTRUMENTS

The mbira (kalimba) is the most important instrument of the Shona people. It is played as a solo instrument for recreation, as well as in an ensemble for rituals.

There are many types of mbira in Africa, with different arrangements of keys and different playing styles. Sometimes the player will give a special name to his mbira and will sing in response to it in the same way he would respond to a person singing a call.

Listen to the tone color of the mbira.

⊚ Hande Hande
2

gankogui

conga drum

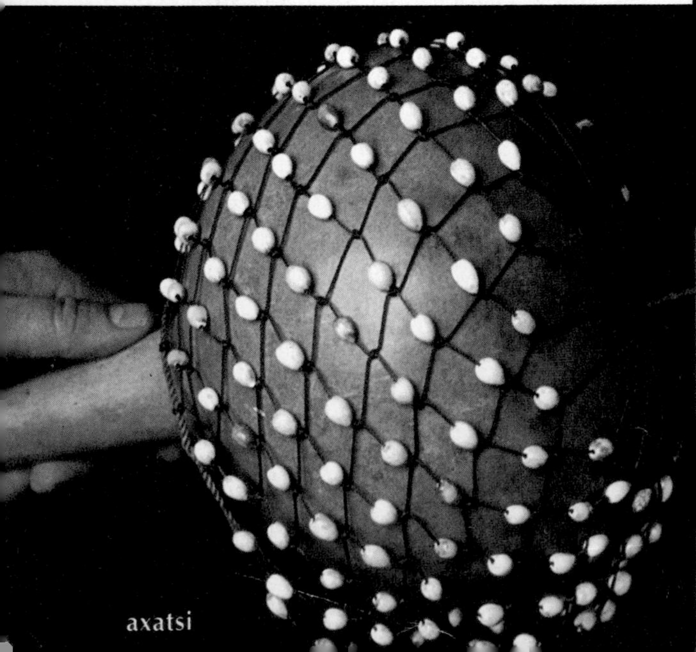

axatsi

MUSIC FOR FOUR VOICES

Shona music often has many voice parts that fit with each other
in the same way that drum patterns in a dance ensemble are
related.

Here is a song, originally sung at a time of great famine, that
has four voice parts. Try to hear the four separate parts and how
they weave together. The notation shows what each group is
singing.

Tarowera

Part 1: Ta - ro - w'ra ku - dya zve Ku - psva - ra _____

Part 2: to _____ Kwa Go - to _____ Kwa Go.

Part 3: Va - no - che - ke - che - ra nde - b'va Ku - ra - pa - hwa - hwa _____

Part 4: Go - mo gu - ru re - mbi - ri Go - mo gu - ru re - mbi - ri

Notice that the parts are written in different clefs—treble for
parts 1–3; bass for part 4. Which part do the low voices follow?

Practice the rhythm pattern on which each part is based.
Play the drum on the counts shown by the enlarged numbers.

1 2 **3** 4 **5** 6 **7** **8** 9

AFRICAN RHYTHM COMPLEX

Chant each line of the following set of numbers. Clap on the large-size numbers only.

1. **1** 2 **3** 4 **5** **6** 7 **8** 9 **10** 11 **12**

2. **1** 2 3 **4** 5 6 **7** 8 9 **10** 11 12

3. **1** 2 **3** **4** **5** **6** **7** **8** **9** **10** **11** **12**

4. **1** **2** **3** **4** 5 6 **7** **8** **9** **10** 11 12

5. 1 2 **3** **4** 5 **6** **7** 8 **9** **10** 11 12

🔵 African Rhythm Complex
2

Choose one line to play over and over as others in the class clap different lines. You hear a combination of rhythm patterns called *polyrhythm*.

POLYRHYTHM

Now look at the notation for the rhythms you clapped. Choose one of the parts to practice.

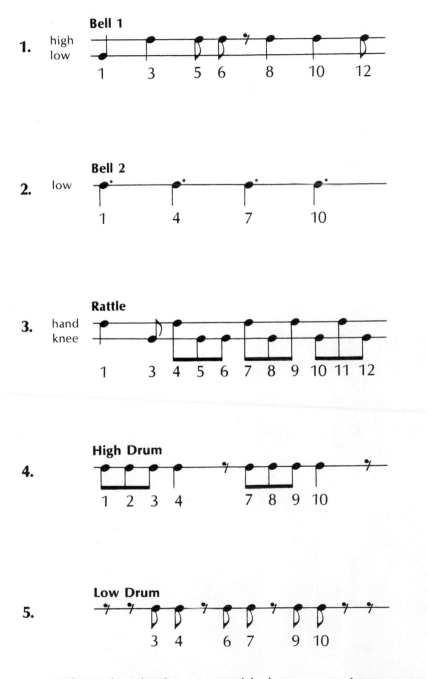

When the rhythms are added one at a time, you will hear polyrhythm in a complex that uses a combination of tone colors.

Experiencing the Arts: Pattern

PATTERNS IN PHOTOGRAPHS AND POETRY

Patterns can be made by lines, shapes, and colors. How many patterns can you find in these photographs?

In "Summer Grass" you can see and hear patterns.

• The word *it* at the beginning of some lines forms a pattern. What other words form a pattern?

• What is the pattern of punctuation in the poem?

• What is the pattern formed by the length of phrases?

Follow the words of the poem as you listen to the recording.

Sandburg: Summer Grass

SUMMER GRASS

Summer grass aches
  and whispers.

It wants something;
it calls out and sings;
it pours out wishes
  to the overhead stars.

The rain hears;
the rain answers;
the rain is slow coming;
the rain wets the face
  of the grass.

Carl Sandburg

PATTERNS IN SONG

In the song "Emma" you can see and hear pattern.

• Notice the rhythm pattern that is repeated in every measure.

• As you listen to the song, find the patterns that are alike in melody as well as rhythm.

Emma
FOLK SONG FROM TRINIDAD AND TOBAGO

USED BY PERMISSION OF DR. J. D. ELDER, PH.D. (PENN. UNIV.), ANTHROPOLOGIST, CHAIRMAN, NATIONAL CULTURAL COUNCIL OF TRINIDAD AND TOBAGO, WEST INDIES.

Em - ma, le' me 'lone, le' me 'lone. Me no mar - ry yet, le' me 'lone.

Em - ma, le' me 'lone, le' me 'lone. Me no mar - ry yet, le' me 'lone.

When me mar - ry, oh, bell go ring. When me mar - ry, oh, shell go blow.

Em - ma, le' me 'lone, le' me 'lone. Me no mar - ry yet, le' me 'lone.

Here is a pattern to play on maracas as others sing the song.

35

PATTERNS IN
PAINTING AND MUSIC

The shapes of the sails create a
pattern in this painting. What
other patterns do you see?

You have seen pattern in
photographs of familiar objects,
in poetry, in a song, and in a
painting. Now hear how pattern
is used in this piece for orchestra.

Listen for the repeated rhythm
pattern and tap it lightly.

Stravinsky: *Agon*, "Bransle Gay"

We can see pattern in painting.

We can hear pattern in music.

PATTERNS IN OUR NATIONAL ANTHEM

You can see patterns every time you look at the American flag.

You can hear patterns every time you sing "The Star-Spangled Banner."

Look at the rhythm pattern made by the words in each color box. Each pattern is repeated in other places in the song. Can you find the repetitions?

The Star-Spangled Banner

WORDS BY FRANCIS SCOTT KEY

MUSIC BY JOHN STAFFORD SMITH

1. Oh,___ say! can you see, by the dawn's ear - ly light, What so
2. On the shore, dim - ly seen through the mists of the deep, Where the
3. Oh,___ thus be it ever when___ free men shall stand Be -

proud - ly we hailed at the twi - light's last gleam - ing, Whose broad
foe's haugh - ty host in dread si - lence re - pos - es, What is
tween their loved homes and the war's des - o - la - tion! Blest with

stripes and bright stars, through the per - il - ous fight, O'er the
that which the breeze, o'er the tow - er - ing steep, As it
vic - t'ry and peace, may the heav'n - res - cued land Praise the

ram - parts we watched were so gal - lant - ly stream - ing? And the
fit - ful - ly blows, half con-ceals, half dis - clos - es? Now it
Pow'r that hath made and pre-served us a na - tion! Then___

rock - ets' red glare, the bombs burst - ing in air, Gave
catch - es the gleam of the morn - ing's first beam, In full
con - quer we must, when our cause it is just, And

proof through the night that our flag was still there. Oh,
glo - ry re - flected now___ shines on the stream; 'Tis the
this be our motto: "In___ God is our trust!" And the

say, does that Star - Span - gled Ban - ner___ yet___ wave___ O'er the
Star - Span - gled Ban - ner, oh, long may___ it___ wave___ O'er the
Star - Span - gled Ban - ner in tri - umph___ shall___ wave___ O'er the

land_____ of the free and the home of the brave?
land_____ of the free and the home of the brave!
land_____ of the free and the home of the brave!

PATTERNS IN MOVEMENT

All the arts use pattern in their own way. In dance the movement of the body creates patterns.

As you listen to this music, clap this rhythm. Listen for the steady beat before starting to clap.

🎵 *Yes Me Siroon*
2

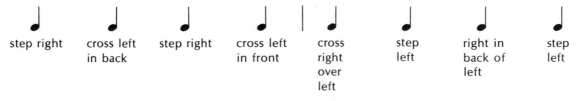

Now show the same pattern with your feet. Join hands and walk in a circle.

right	left	right	left	right	left

Still holding hands, face the center of the circle and move sideways to the right.

step right	cross left in back	step right	cross left in front	cross right over left	step left	right in back of left	step left

After practicing, dance the pattern with a group, moving in a circle. Your movement in a circle created another kind of pattern, called a *floor pattern*.

📖 For other movement activities, see pp. 237–250.

40

WHAT DO YOU HEAR? 1: Rhythm Patterns

Point to the notation that shows the rhythm pattern you hear.

Using What You Know About Form

Sounds are not music until they are organized in some way. The organization of a piece of music—the way it is put together—is its form.

On the following pages you will learn some more about the forms of music.

Form is all around us. Our lives would be confused and bewildering if we did not organize things. We need to give form to our world.

What gives a sense of order—form—to these things?
Use such words in your discussion as:

patterns	variations	balance and imbalance
contrast	repetition	expected and unexpected

REPETITION AND CONTRAST

Many songs are "put together" with sections that repeat and contrast. Follow the music of "Lazybones" as you listen to the recording. The letters A and B in the score will help you hear the beginning and ending of sections. Which section repeats, A or B?

Lazybones

WORDS AND MUSIC BY JOHNNY MERCER AND HOAGY CARMICHAEL

La - zy - bones, sleep-in' in the sun, How you 'spec' to get your

day's work done? Nev - er get your day's work done,

Sleep - in' in the noon - day sun. La - zy - bones,

sleep-in' in the shade, How you 'spec' to get your corn - meal made?

Nev-er get your corn-meal made, Sleep-in' in the eve - nin' shade.

When 'ta - ters need spray - in' I bet you keep pray - in' the

bugs fall off of the vine. And when you go fish-in' I

bet you keep wish-in' the fish won"t grab at your line.

Ⓐ La — zy-bones, loaf-in' thru the day, How you 'spec' to make a

dime that way? Nev-er make a dime that way, (well, look-y here, ___)

He nev-er heared a word I say!

MAKE A SOUND, MAKE A MOVEMENT

Make up a set of sounds and movements to show the contrast between section A and section B. Here are some suggestions.

Section A: Make four different sounds, one for each of the four beats in each measure. For example, snap fingers, tap foot, tap windowpane, scrape window blind.

Section B: Make four different motions, one for each of the four beats in each measure: wave right hand, wave left hand, shrug right shoulder, shrug left shoulder.

FOLLOW THE DIAGRAM

Follow the diagram as you listen to this song to hear which section repeats and which section is a contrast.

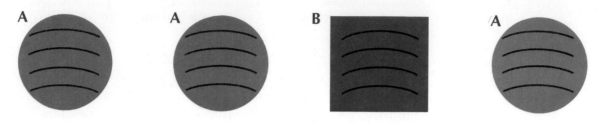

A   A   B   A

How many phrases are shown in the diagram for each section?

Mountain Sound

1972 DAVID McHUGH

WORDS AND MUSIC BY DAVID McHUGH

1. When the sky is clear at sun - down,
2. Hear the owl a - soft - ly call - in',
4. Wake up ear - ly with the sun - rise,

And the stars start a - com - in'____ round,____
Hear the bob - cat____ in the ____ tree,____
Nev - er could when I lived in ____ town,____

Look out yon - der to the moun - tain,
While the night is soft - ly fall - in',
But I nev - er had the peace of mind

Fine

Lis - ten to that moun - tain sound.
Moun - tain sound is call - in' me.
Of liv - ing with that moun - tain sound.

A SONG IN TWO SECTIONS (A) [B]

Read the words of this song, then explain what you think the title means.

Look at the melody notes in the color boxes. In which section do the notes move upward? Downward?

It's a Small World

WORDS AND MUSIC BY RICHARD M. SHERMAN AND ROBERT B. SHERMAN

© 1963 WONDERLAND MUSIC CO., INC. REPRINTED BY PERMISSION

(A) VERSE   G   D₇

1. It's   a   world   of   laugh - ter,   a   world   of   tears;
2. There   is   just   one   moon   and   one   gold - en   sun,

D₇   G

It's   a   world   of   hopes   and   a   world   of   fears.
And   a   smile   means   friend - ship   to   ev - 'ry - one.

G   G₇   C

There's   so   much   that   we   share   that   it's   time   we're   a - ware,
Though   the   moun - tains   di - vide   and   the   o - ceans   are   wide,

C   D₇   G

It's   a   small   world   af - ter   all.

[B] REFRAIN
G   D₇

It's   a   small   world   af - ter   all,

It's a small world af - ter all,

It's a small world af - ter all,

It's a small, small world. _____

TRY THIS: One group can sing the A section, and at the same time another group can sing the melody of the B section.

WHAT DO YOU HEAR? 2: Form

These pieces have two sections. The form is AB.
Choose the word or words that tell how the sections contrast.

1	MAJOR-MINOR	METER	Kingsley: *Piece in Two Meters*
2	RHYTHM	METER	"Mineira de Minas"
3	TONE COLOR	MAJOR-MINOR	Mozart: *Rondo alla turca*
4	MELODY	METER	"It's a Small World"
5	MAJOR-MINOR	METER	"El Capotín"

A SONG IN THREE SECTIONS Ⓐ ⃞B △C

How do you think this work song should be sung? The words may give you a clue.

As you listen to the recording, decide which of the three contrasting sections you will accompany. You will find suggestions for added parts on p. 51.

Tzena, Tzena

FOLK SONG FROM ISRAEL   ENGLISH WORDS BY PHYLLIS RESNICK

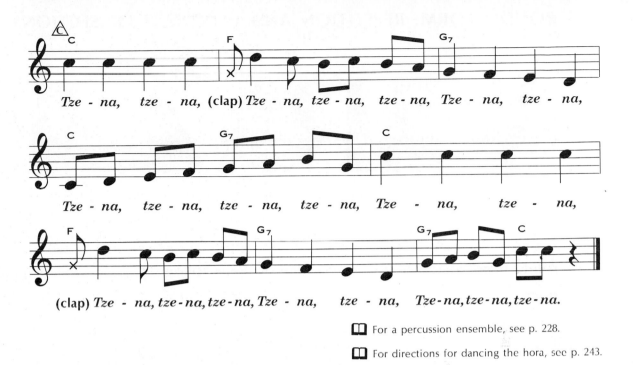

Tze - na, tze - na, (clap) Tze - na, tze - na, tze - na, Tze - na, tze - na,

Tze - na, tze - na, tze - na, tze - na, Tze - na, tze - na,

(clap) Tze - na, tze - na, tze - na, Tze - na, tze - na, Tze - na, tze - na, tze - na.

📖 For a percussion ensemble, see p. 228.

📖 For directions for dancing the hora, see p. 243.

ADD A PART

Woodblock

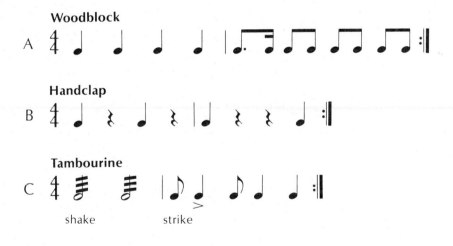

Handclap

Tambourine

shake   strike

This Autoharp part can be used to accompany all three sections.

Autoharp

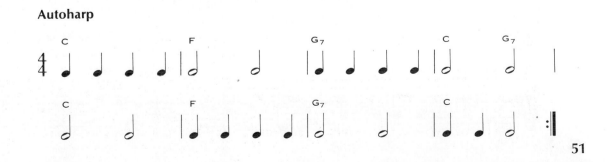

RONDO FORM: REPETITION AND CONTRAST OF SECTIONS

The diagram at the top of the page will help you discover how the sections in a piece of music are put together to create a rondo form. Study the diagram and answer the following questions:

• Which section repeats?

• How many contrasting sections does the diagram show?

• Which section do you find at the end of the diagram?

CALL CHART 2: Rondo   Mouret: *Symphonic de fanfares*, "Rondeau"   2

This piece for trumpet, organ, and timpani is in rondo form.
Follow the chart as you listen. It will help you hear what is
going on as the music goes along.

Another time, try following the notation of the music in each
section.

1	SECTION A	TRUMPET SOLO; FOUR PHRASES— PHRASES 1 AND 3 ARE EXACTLY ALIKE, PHRASES 2 AND 4 ARE NEARLY ALIKE.
2	SECTION B	NO TRUMPET; TWO PHRASES, ALIKE IN RHYTHM AND MELODY
3	SECTION A	PHRASES 3 AND 4 ONLY
4	SECTION C	NO TRUMPET; LONG AND SHORT PHRASES
5	SECTION A	SAME AS NUMBER 1

A DANCE IN THREE SECTIONS

You have played, sung, and listened to music that is "put together" in three sections. Listen to the recording of *Tarantella*, a folk dance tune from Italy, to hear three contrasting sections.

◉ *Tarantella*
3

The movements in the folk dance
show the contrast between the sections.

DANCE

Partners stand side by side in a set
of 8, as shown in the diagram.

Section A

Keeping the same places in the set, all run forward around the room and back to place. Try to get back to place when the repeat of Section A comes to an end (16 measures in all).

Section B

Partners face each other in the set.

Phrase 1 (2 measures): All run forward four steps, passing right shoulders with partner.

Phrase 2 (2 measures): All take four running steps in place, turning around to face partner.

Phrase 3: same as phrase 1.

Phrase 4: same as phrase 2.

Section C

Partners still facing, hands on hips.

Phrase 1 (4 measures): While hopping on left foot, point right toe to front, then to the side—front, side, front, side, throughout the phrase.

Phrase 2 (4 measures): Join hands and change places in set.

Repeat phrase 1, but hop on right foot.

Repeat phrase 2, but join hands and return to place.

Banana Boat Loaders

FOLK SONG FROM JAMAICA

FROM FOLK SONGS OF JAMAICA COMPILED BY TOM MURRAY. COPYRIGHT 1952 BY THE OXFORD UNIVERSITY PRESS, LONDON. USED BY PERMISSION.

Listen for the contrasting sections in this work song from
Jamaica. Join in on the chorus parts when you can.

Day oh! Day oh! Day is break - ing, I wan-na go home.

1. Come, Mis - ter Tal - ly - man, come tal - ly my ba -
2. Came here for work, I did - n't come here for to

nan - as. Day is break - ing, I wan - na go home.
i - dle. Day is break - ing, I wan - na go home.

3. Three han', four han', five han', Bunch! Six han', seven han',

eight han', Bunch! Day is break - ing, I wan - na go home.

4. So check them, and check them but check with cau - tion.
5. My back is a - break - ing with bare ex - haus - tion.

Day is break - ing, I wan - na go home, wan - na go home.

55

CALL AND RESPONSE

In this song, the leader "lines out" a phrase and other singers respond by repeating the phrase. Join in on the chorus parts as you listen to the recording.

Long John   BLUES SONG

SOLO   CHORUS

With his shin - y blade,___ *With his shin - y blade,___*

Got it in his hand,___ *Got it in his hand,___*

Gon - na chop out the live oaks, *Gon - na chop out the live oaks,*

That are in this land,___ *That are in this land.___*

He's Long John,___ *He's Long John,___* He's long gone,___

He's long gone,___ He's gone, gone,___ *He's gone, gone,___*

Like a tur-key in the corn,___ *Like a tur-key in the corn,*___

With his long clothes on,___ *With his long clothes on,*___

He's long gone,___ He's long gone,___ He's long gone,___

*He's long gone,*_____ He's gone, He's long gone.___

Can you find other places in the song where the notes match those shown in each color box?

Play these patterns on bells or piano. Can you hear the contrast between the sound of major and minor?

major

B   D   G
He's long gone, __

minor

B♭   D   G
He's gone, gone, _____

Chant the rhythm of the words in these patterns. Can you hear the contrast between no syncopation and syncopation?

no syncopation

with his shin - y blade,___

syncopation

Gon - na chop out   the live oaks,

TRACING PHRASES

As you listen to the recording, trace the length of each phrase
by moving your hand in the air. How many phrases are there?
Do any of the phrases repeat?

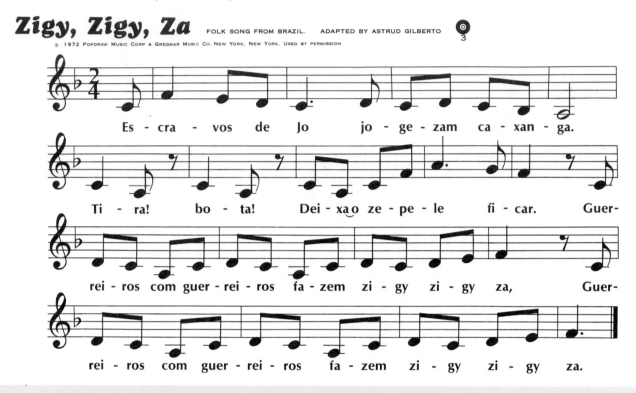

Zigy, Zigy, Za FOLK SONG FROM BRAZIL. ADAPTED BY ASTRUD GILBERTO

© 1972 POPDRAW MUSIC CORP & GREGMAR MUSIC CO. NEW YORK, NEW YORK. USED BY PERMISSION

Es - cra - vos de Jo jo - ge - zam ca - xan - ga.

Ti - ra! bo - ta! Dei - xa o ze - pe - le fi - car. Guer-

rei - ros com guer - rei - ros fa - zem zi - gy zi - gy za, Guer-

rei - ros com guer - rei - ros fa - zem zi - gy zi - gy za.

CALL CHART 3: Phrases

Listen to another arrangement of "Zigy, Zigy, Za." Notice
especially what happens at calls 4, 6, and 8.

1	INTRODUCTION: PERCUSSION, VOICE IN BACKGROUND
2	VOICE ENTERS, CHANTING RHYTHM OF SONG
3	VOCAL SECTION
4	CONTRASTING INSTRUMENTAL SECTION
5	VOCAL SECTION
6	CONTRASTING INSTRUMENTAL SECTION
7	VOCAL SECTION
8	CONTRASTING INSTRUMENTAL SECTION

ADDING CONTRAST AT THE KEYBOARD

In *Call Chart 3* you heard an arrangement of "Zigy, Zigy, Za" that contrasts vocal sections with instrumental sections. When you listen to the recording again, add your own piano part during the instrumental sections—at calls 4, 6, and 8.

Choose one of the patterns below to play in any register of the piano—high, middle, or low.

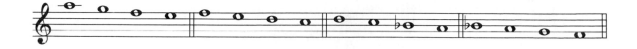

Play each note of the pattern you choose eight times, using the index finger of either hand.

Be ready to play the pattern over as many times as you hear it on the recording in each contrasting instrumental section.

The four patterns can be played at the same time. To do this, team up with three friends.

When the tones of the four patterns are sounded together, they create harmony. The horizontal and vertical lines show the patterns sounding together.

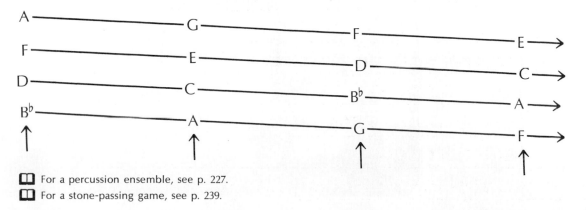

📖 For a percussion ensemble, see p. 227.
📖 For a stone-passing game, see p. 239.

Experiencing the Arts: Form

PARTS WORK TOGETHER IN PAINTING

Can you name some of the parts of a bicycle? Of a car? Of a motorcycle?

All the parts work together to make the whole bicycle, car, or motorcycle. Each part adds something important.

The arts are made of parts that work together.

Some of the same parts—things you can see—are used in these two paintings. Can you find them?

- a foreground (in front) and a background
- darker colors against lighter colors
- strong vertical (up and down) shapes
- strong horizontal (side to side) shapes or lines across the bottom and across the middle
- a round, white, active shape in the same position in each painting
- a large rounded yellow shape in the same position in each painting

The two paintings have a similar form (arrangement of parts), yet each has its own special look.

PARTS WORK TOGETHER IN POETRY

In poetry, some of the parts that make up the whole are images (mind pictures), rhymes (although not every poem uses rhyme), length of lines, and rhythm of the words.

Look for these things in this poem:
- words that give you images
- rhyme
- arrangement of long and short lines
- the rhythm—flow—of the words

FOURTH OF JULY NIGHT

The little boat at anchor
in black water sat murmuring
to the tall black sky.
* * *

A white sky bomb fizzed on a black line.
A rocket hissed its red signature into the west.
Now a shower of Chinese fire alphabets,
a cry of flower pots broken in flames,
a long curve to a purple spray,
three violet balloons—

Drips of seaweed tangled in gold,
shimmering symbols of mixed numbers,
tremulous arrangements of cream gold folds
of a bride's wedding gown—
* * *

A few sky bombs spoke their pieces,
then velvet dark.

The little boat at anchor
in black water sat murmuring
to the tall black sky.

Carl Sandburg

PARTS WORK TOGETHER IN MUSIC

In music, the parts that work together to form a whole are sounds. Sounds can get louder or softer. They can go slower or faster. They can change tone color and density, get higher and lower, repeat and contrast.

How many of these parts can you hear working together as you listen? The chart below will help you identify the parts within a whole piece.

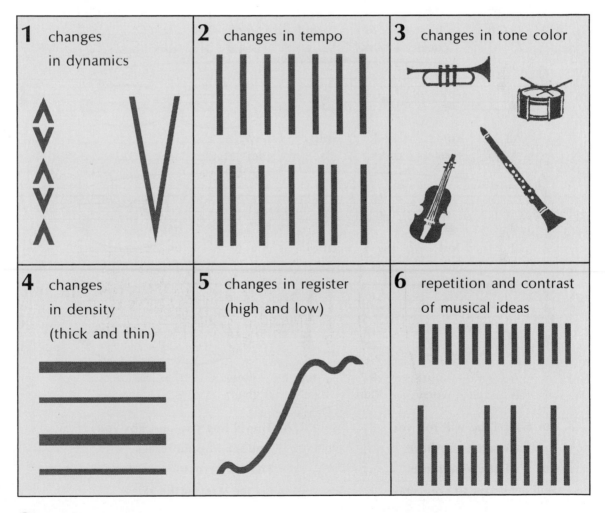

1 changes in dynamics

2 changes in tempo

3 changes in tone color

4 changes in density (thick and thin)

5 changes in register (high and low)

6 repetition and contrast of musical ideas

Stravinsky: *Rite of Spring,* "Evocation of Ancestors" and "Ritual of Ancestors"

In every art, the whole is formed from parts working together. We notice the parts, but we also experience the work as a whole.

More About Form

FOLLOW THE PHRASE LINES

As you sing this familiar American folk song, trace the rise and fall of the phrase lines with your finger. This will help you feel the length of each phrase.

On Top of Old Smoky   FOLK SONG FROM KENTUCKY

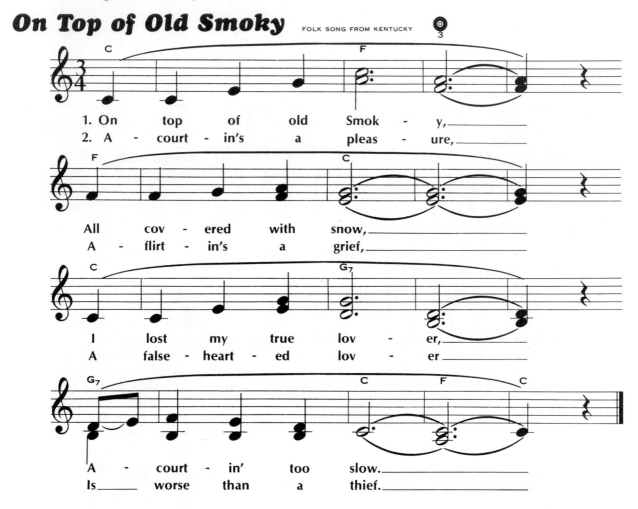

1. On   top   of   old   Smok - y,_____
2. A - court - in's   a   pleas - ure,_____

All   cov - ered   with   snow,_____
A - flirt - in's   a   grief,_____

I   lost   my   true   lov - er,_____
A   false - heart - ed   lov - er _____

A - court - in'   too   slow._____
Is_____ worse   than   a   thief._____

3. For a thief, he will rob you
   And take what you have,
   But a falsehearted lover
   Will send you to your grave.

4. They'll hug you and kiss you,
   And tell you more lies
   Than the crossties on the railroad,
   Or the stars in the skies.

5. Come, all you young maidens,
   And listen to me,
   Never place your affections
   On a green willow tree.

6. The leaves they will wither,
   The roots they will die,
   You'll all be forsaken,
   And never know why.

For recorder parts, see p. 209.

FOLLOW THE PHRASE DIAGRAM

Compare the phrase lines in this diagram. How does the diagram show what you hear in the song below?

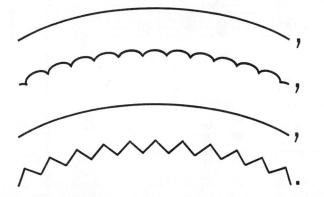

He's Got the Whole World in His Hands

BLACK SPIRITUAL

1. He's got the whole world___ in his hands,___
2. He's got the wind and rain___ in his hands,___
3. He's got both you and me___ in his hands,___

He's got the whole world___ in his hands,___
He's got the wind and rain___ in his hands,___
He's got both you and me___ in his hands,___

He's got the whole world___ in his hands,___
He's got the wind and rain___ in his hands,___
He's got both you and me___ in his hands,___

He's got the whole world in his hands.___
He's got the whole world in his hands.___
He's got the whole world in his hands.___

CREATE A PHRASE DIAGRAM

Deep Blue Sea

AMERICAN FOLK SONG

phrase 1

1. Deep blue sea, ba - by, deep blue sea,

phrase 2

Deep blue sea, ba - by, deep blue sea,

phrase 3

Deep blue sea, ba - by, deep blue sea,

phrase 4

It was Wil - lie___ what got drown - ded

In the deep blue sea.

2. Low'r him down with a golden chain, (*3 times*)
   It was Willie . . .

3. Dig his grave with a silver spade, (*3 times*)

4. Wrap him up in a silken shroud, (*3 times*)

5. Golden sun bring him back to me, (*3 times*)

- Which phrases have the same melody?
- Which have the same rhythm?
- How is phrase 4 a contrast?
- In which phrases do you find the same order of Autoharp chords?

Make up your own diagram that shows what you have learned about the phrases in "Deep Blue Sea."

For a drum part, see p. 230.

CALL CHART 4: Form ⊙₃ *Anonymous: Trotto*

Diagrams can help you to train your ears. What does the diagram in this call chart tell you about the form of *Trotto,* a piece composed about 600 years ago?

At call number 1, Introduction, there are drum beats and a trombone "call" of a few notes. (The call is shown by ∿ on the chart.) Notice how the call connects phrases throughout the piece.

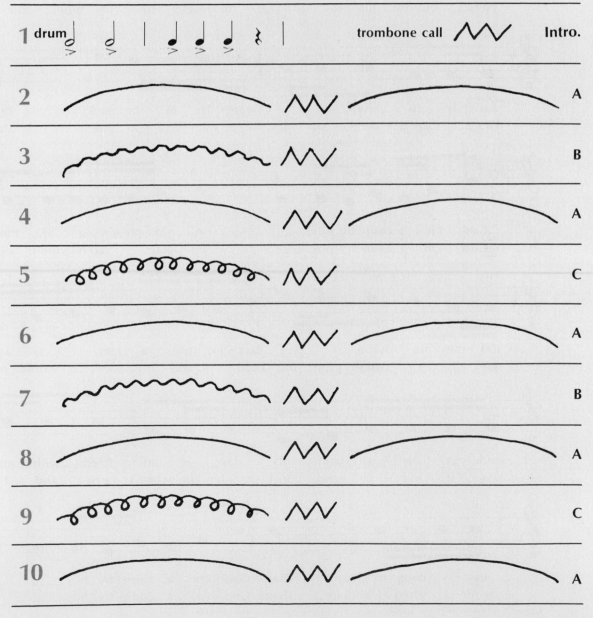

Thank God, I'm a Country Boy

WORDS AND MUSIC BY JOHN MARTIN SOMMERS

1. Well, life on a farm is kind-a laid back, ain't much an old coun-try boy like me can't hack. It's ear-ly to rise, ear-ly in the sack; Thank God, I'm a coun-try boy. A sim-ple kind-a life nev-er did me no harm, Rais-in' me a fam-i-ly and work-in' on a farm. My days are all filled with an eas-y coun-try charm; Thank God, I'm a coun-try boy.

2. When the work's all done and the sun's settin' low I pull out my fid-dle and I ro-sin up my bow. But the kids are a-sleep so I keep it kind-a low; Thank God, I'm a coun-try boy. I'd play "Sal-ly Goodin'" all day if I could, but the Lord and my wife would-n't take it ver-y good. So I fid-dle when I can and I work when I should; Thank God, I'm a coun-try boy.

B REFRAIN

Well, I got me a fine wife, I got me old fid - dle. When the

sun's com - in' up I got cakes___ on the grid - dle; And

life ain't no - thin' but a fun - ny, fun - ny rid - dle; Thank

God, I'm a coun - try boy.___

3. I wouldn't trade my life for diamonds or jewels,
   I never was one of them money hungry fools.
   I'd rather have my fiddle and my farmin' tools;
   Thank God, I'm a country boy.
   Yeah, city folk drivin' in a black limousine,
   A lotta sad people thinkin' that's mighty keen.
   Well, folks, let me tell you now exactly what I mean;
   Thank God, I'm a country boy. *Refrain*

4. Well, my fiddle was my daddy's till the day he died,
   And he took me by the hand and held me close to his side.
   He said, "Live a good life and play my fiddle with pride,
   And thank God you're a country boy."
   My daddy taught me young how to hunt and how to whittle,
   He taught me how to work and play a tune on the fiddle.
   He taught me how to love and how to give just a little;
   Thank God, I'm a country boy. *Refrain*

You can show the form of this song through dance. Use
movement to show sections A and B and the phrases in each
section.

For a percussion ensemble, see p. 231.
For another square dance, see p. 247.

Pay Me My Money Down

SLAVE SONG FROM THE GEORGIA
SEA ISLANDS COLLECTED AND
ADAPTED BY LYDIA A. PARRISH

TRO—® COPYRIGHT 1942 AND RENEWED 1970 HOLLIS MUSIC, INC. NEW YORK, N.Y.
USED BY PERMISSION.

PHRASE ENDINGS—CADENCES

Think of some special days and special events that you look forward to. You expect something to happen. This feeling of expectation is created in music, too.

As you sing this song, notice that the first three phrases in each section seem unfinished, or incomplete—something more is needed to complete the musical thought. The last phrase of each section seems finished, or complete.

The ending of a phrase is called a *cadence*.

1. I thought I heard the cap - tain say,
"Pay me my mon - ey down,___
To - mor - row is our sail - ing day,___
Pay me my mon - ey down."___

REFRAIN

"Pay___ me,___ oh, pay___ me,___
Pay me my mon - ey down,___
Pay me or go to jail,___
Pay me my mon - ey down."___

2. As soon as the boat was
      clear of the bar,
   "Pay me my money down,"
   He knocked me down with
      the end of a spar,
   "Pay me my money down."
      Refrain

3. Well, I wish I was Mr.
      Steven's son,
   "Pay me my money down,"
   Sit on the bank and watch
      the work done,
   "Pay me my money down."
      Refrain

For a guitar part, see p. 192.   For recorder parts, see pp. 210 and 211.

STRONG AND WEAK CADENCE

As in "Pay Me My Money Down," the first three phrases of this song seem unfinished, or incomplete. A sense of expectation continues throughout the song until the final strong cadence.

Streets of Laredo
AMERICAN COWBOY SONG

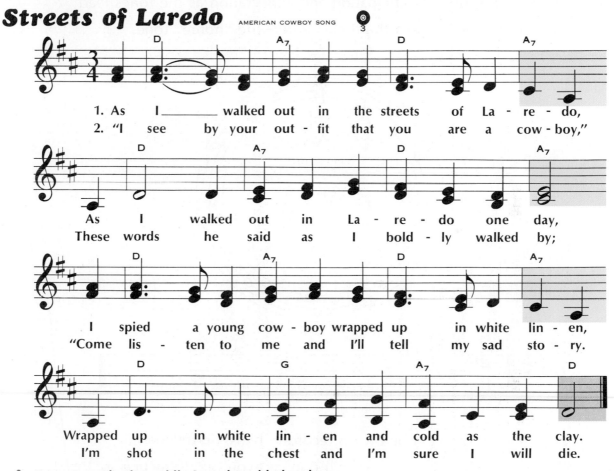

1. As I _____ walked out in the streets of La - re - do,
2. "I see by your out - fit that you are a cow - boy,"

As I walked out in La - re - do one day,
These words he said as I bold - ly walked by;

I spied a young cow - boy wrapped up in white lin - en,
"Come lis - ten to me and I'll tell my sad sto - ry.

Wrapped up in white lin - en and cold as the clay.
I'm shot in the chest and I'm sure I will die.

3. "Now once in the saddle I used to ride handsome,
   'A handsome young cowboy' is what they would say.
   I'd ride into town and go down to the card-house,
   But I'm shot in the chest and I'm dying today.

4. "Go run to the spring for a cup of cold water
   To cool down my fever," the young cowboy said.
   But when I returned, his poor soul had departed,
   And I wept when I saw the young cowboy was dead.

5. We'll bang the drum slowly and play the fife lowly,
   We'll play the dead march as we bear him along.
   We'll go to the graveyard and lay the sod o'er him;
   He was a young cowboy, but he had done wrong.

For guitar parts, see p. 194.

71

ANTICIPATION AND EXPECTATION

3 Pachelbel: *Canon in D Major*

In this music, you will hear the lowest part, called a *ground bass,*
repeat over and over throughout the piece. Follow the part in the circle
to feel the sense of anticipation and expectation as the tones lead
away from and back to the tonal center—the "home" tone.

Play one of the parts below on recorder, bells, or keyboard
throughout the recording. Which one can you play? Practice so
the parts can be played together.

72

Now listen to a rock composition. The sense of anticipation and expectation is created by the pattern of chords. Follow the chords as they lead from one to another until the home chord is reached.

Striano, Luccisano, Gentile:
There's a Moon Out Tonight

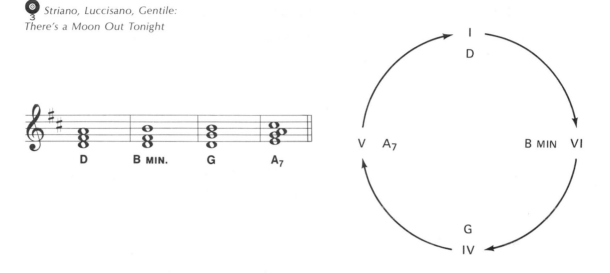

In this music from India, a sense of expectation is created by the *tala*, or rhythm pattern. It uses a cycle of 7 beats described on p. 13.

Raga Maru-Bihag

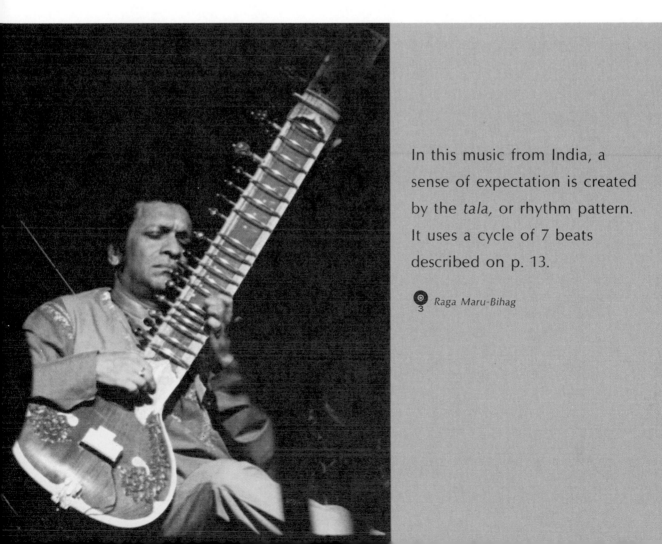

WHAT DO YOU HEAR? 3: Phrases ⊙

I. Listen for phrases that repeat or that contrast. At numbers 3, 4, 5, and 6 decide whether the phrase is a repeat of what you heard at number 2 (Phrase A) or is a contrasting phrase, B.

1	*INTRODUCTION*	
2	*PHRASE A*	
3	*PHRASE A REPEATED*	*CONTRASTING PHRASE B*
4	*PHRASE A REPEATED*	*CONTRASTING PHRASE B*
5	*PHRASE A REPEATED*	*CONTRASTING PHRASE B*
6	*PHRASE A REPEATED*	*CONTRASTING PHRASE B*

Anonymous: *Trotto*

II. How many phrases do you hear in this music? Choose the correct number for each piece.

1	*1*	*2*	*3*	*4*	*5*	Bach: *Cantata 79*, "Chorale" (excerpt)
2	*1*	*2*	*3*	*4*	*5*	Barber: *Adagio for Strings* (excerpt)
3	*1*	*2*	*3*	*4*	*5*	Polka (excerpt)
4	*1*	*2*	*3*	*4*	*5*	Hallelujah (excerpt)

III. When you hear a number called, decide whether it comes in the middle of a phrase or at the end of a phrase. Choose the correct answer.

1	*MIDDLE*	*END*
2	*MIDDLE*	*END*
3	*MIDDLE*	*END*
4	*MIDDLE*	*END*
5	*MIDDLE*	*END*
6	*MIDDLE*	*END*

Haydn: *Divertimento*, Movement 3

CADENCE—STRONG OR WEAK?

Listen to the recording, then draw a phrase plan for this song.
Use a comma to show a weak cadence; a period to show a
strong cadence.

Thanksgiving Chorale

MUSIC BY J. L. STEINER · · · WORDS BY JOHN ARLOTT

"GOD'S FARM" BY JOHN ARLOTT. REPRINTED BY PERMISSION OF JOHN ARLOTT

1. God, whose farm____ is all cre - a - tion,

Take the grat - i - tude we give;

Take the fin - est of our har - vest,

Crops____ we____ grow that____ men may live.

2. Take our ploughing, seeding, reaping,
   Hopes and fears of sun and rain,
   All our thinking, planning, waiting,
   Ripened in this fruit and grain.

3. All our labor, all our watching,
   All our calendar of care,
   In these crops of your creation,
   Take, O God: they are our prayer.

If you can play low D, G, A, B, C, high D, and high E on the
recorder, try playing the melody.

If you are a beginner on the recorder, try playing the
countermelody.

Recorder or bells

FOLLOW THE DIAGRAM

Sounds are not music until they are organized in some way—until they are given a form. What can you discover about the form of this song by following the diagram?

Winter Wonderland

MUSIC BY FELIX BERNARD   WORDS BY DICK SMITH

© 1934 BY BREGMAN, VOCCO & CONN, INC. COPYRIGHT RENEWED 1961. ALL RIGHTS RESERVED. USED BY PERMISSION.

1. Sleigh-bells ring, are you lis-t'nin'? In the lane snow is
2. Gone a-way is the blue-bird, Here to stay is a
3. When it snows, ain't it thrill-in'? Tho' your nose gets a

glis-t'nin', A beau-ti-ful sight,___ We're hap-py to-night,___
new bird, He's sing-ing a song___ as we go a-long,___
chill-in', We'll frol-ic and play___ the Es-ki-mo way,___

Walk-in' in a win-ter won-der-land! land!

In the mead-ow we can build a snow-man,

And pre-tend that he's a cir-cus clown; We'll have lots of fun with Mis-ter

Snow-man, Un-til the oth-er kid-dies knock 'im down!

(To verse 3)

Simple Gifts (A Simple Gift)

WORDS AND MUSIC BY ROD McKUEN

Draw your own diagram to show the form of "Simple Gifts."

Though the gift be small and sim - ple, if the wish is
Let it be a sim - ple gift then, if the wish is

wide, Just the sim - ple gift of giv - ing
wide, Just the sim - ple gift of giv - ing

makes you warm in - side.___ Though the thought is
makes you warm in - side.___

ev - er fleet - ing, if a thought at all,

Re - mem - ber___ all the might - y big things start - ed out as small.___

So if you've a gift worth giv - ing,

let it be your smile.___ Let it be a

kind - ly word___ that makes the stran - ger stop a - while.

Careers in Music: Teach

A music teacher may be involved with music as a composer, a performer, a conductor, a listener. But the unique responsibility of the teacher is to share musical knowledge with others.

For someone who happens to like both music and people, being a music teacher is "having a good thing going."

CONDUCT AN INTERVIEW

Interview one of the music teachers in your school or in the community. Here are some questions you might ask.

1 *WHAT MADE YOU DECIDE TO TEACH MUSIC?*

2 *HOW DID YOU PREPARE TO TEACH MUSIC?*

3 *WHAT SPECIAL AREA OF MUSIC DO YOU TEACH?*

4 *BESIDES TEACHING, WHAT OTHER MUSICAL ROLES ARE YOU INVOLVED WITH?*

5 *WHAT DO YOU FIND REWARDING ABOUT TEACHING MUSIC?*

6 *WHAT ARE THE PROBLEMS OF BEING A MUSIC TEACHER?*

7 *CAN YOU THINK OF A SPECIAL INCIDENT THAT HAS HAPPENED IN YOUR TEACHING?*

Using What You Know About Tone Color

Sounds make music. Our world is filled with sounds, some natural, some from instruments invented to make sounds. This section will review some musical sounds— tone colors—that you know and add a few you might not know.

Words, words, words. Just as music must have sounds, or tone colors, poetry must have words. The poet takes words and organizes them so they feel right together. What are some ways this poet organized his material—his words?

head bed city stone lights morning song sings evening wings

CITY

In the morning the city
Spreads its wings
Making a song
In stone that sings.

In the evening the city
Goes to bed
Hanging lights
About its head.

Langston Hughes

Music must have sounds—
tone colors.

Poetry must have words.

Every art must have its basic
materials.

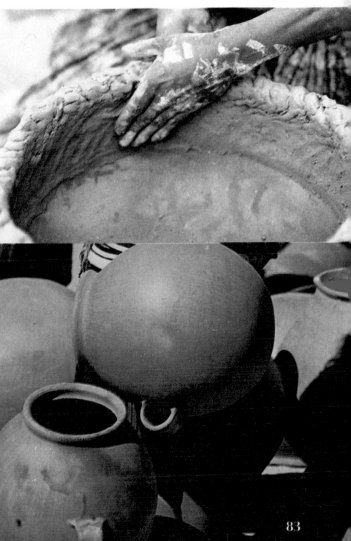

THE SOUND OF PERCUSSION

The percussion instruments used in the recording of this calypso
song from Jamaica add a special flavor to the performance.

As you are learning the song, take turns making up an
accompaniment on bongo drums, maracas, claves, or guiro.

Water Come a Me Eye

FOLK SONG FROM JAMAICA

FROM FOLK SONGS OF JAMAICA (TOM MURRAY), COPYRIGHT 1952 BY THE OXFORD UNIVERSITY PRESS, LONDON. USED BY PERMISSION.

Practice one of these percussion parts and play along with the recording of "Water Come a Me Eye." Then organize a percussion group and play all three parts to accompany the singing.

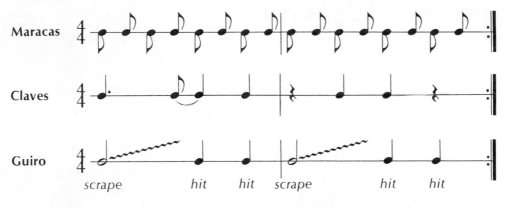

Maracas

Claves

Guiro

scrape   hit   hit   scrape   hit   hit

PUT IT ALL TOGETHER

• Add the tone color of the Autoharp or guitar, playing harmony.

• If you play recorder, try playing the melody.

Practice your part alone before playing with others. When you are ready to perform, choose a leader to set a tempo and to start the group.

Listen to each part as you play so all the parts will *blend* (sound well together).

For a recorder ensemble, see p. 220.
For guitar fingerings, see p. 204.

CLAVES
TAMBOURINE
COWBELL
WOODBLOCK
DRUM

Try using different percussion instruments to accompany "The Hammer Song." Play the rhythm of the words, or play one of these patterns throughout the song.

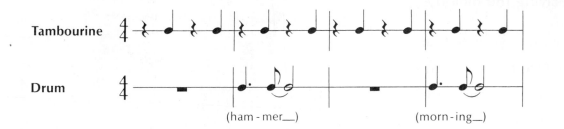

Tambourine

Drum

(ham-mer___)   (morn-ing___)

The Hammer Song

WORDS AND MUSIC BY LEE HAYS AND PETE SEEGER
TRO— Copyright 1958 & 1962 LUDLOW MUSIC, INC., New York, N.Y. Used by permission

1. If   I   had   a   ham - mer,_____
2. If   I   had   a   bell,_____

I'd   ham - mer   in   the   morn - ing,____
I'd   ring   it   in   the   morn - ing,____

86

3. If I had a song, I'd sing it in the morning,
   I'd sing it in the evening all over this land;
   I'd sing out danger, I'd sing out a warning,
   I'd sing out love between my brothers and
     my sisters
   All over this land.

4. Well, I got a hammer and I got a bell,
   And I got a song to sing all over this land;
   It's the hammer of justice,
     it's the bell of freedom,
   It's the song about love between
     my brothers and my sisters
   All over this land.

For a percussion ensemble, see p. 232.
For guitar fingerings, see p. 204.

THE RECORDER

The photographs show the notes used in this piece for recorder.
If you already know them, you are ready to play. If not, take
time to practice the fingerings for B, A, and G.

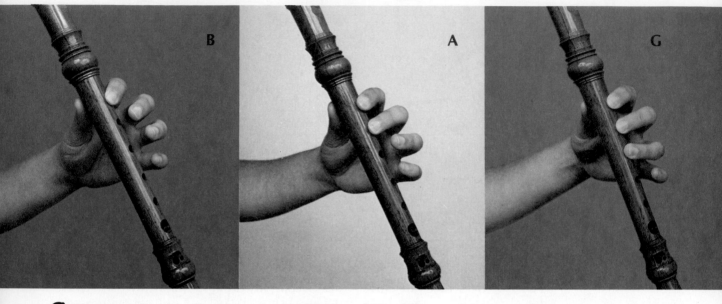

B   A   G

Caravan   MUSIC BY HELMUT BORNEFELD

"VIER LEICHTE STUCKE" FROM 25 EASY PIECES FOR SOPRANO RECORDER AND PIANO. USED BY PERMISSION OF BELWIN-MILLS PUBLISHING CORP. AS SOLE AGENTS FOR EDWIN F. KALMUS & CO., INC.

Ask a friend who plays the piano to practice the part included
in your teacher's book. Add its tone color to the performance.

Listen to the tone color of recorders in this music. What
percussion instruments are added?

 Anonymous: *Five Villancicos,* "Pase el Agoa"

THE GUITAR

This page introduces you to an easy chord, E minor. Look at the photograph to help you place the 2nd and 3rd fingers of your left hand on the strings.

Which strings will you use? How far up on the strings will your fingers go? Look at the diagram below to find the answers.

The 2nd and 3rd fingers are on the A and D strings between the 1st and 2nd frets.

To accompany this song, strum downward across the strings with the thumb of your right hand where you see the stroke (/).

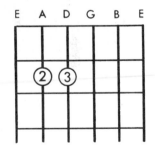

E MINOR

Shalom Chaverim   FOLK ROUND FROM ISRAEL

Sha-lom, cha-ver-im! Sha-lom, cha-ver-im! Sha-lom, sha-lom! Le-

hit - ra - ot, le - hit - ra - ot, Sha-lom, sha - lom.

Other songs using the E minor chord are found on pp. 190 and 191.

89

YOUR VOICE

Your voice has its own tone color, whether you whisper, speak, shout, or sing. Choose one of your favorite songs to sing as an example of your singing voice.

Now use your voice in a different way. Practice the first line of *Sound Piece 2*, which continues throughout the piece as an *ostinato*. Add the other lines when you can.

SOUND PIECE 2: Mouth Sounds   Doris Hays

By Doris Hays © 1973 Tallapoosa Music

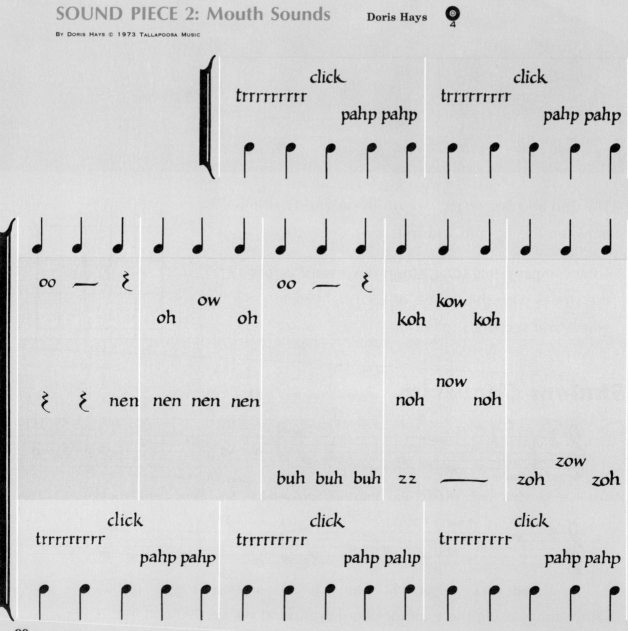

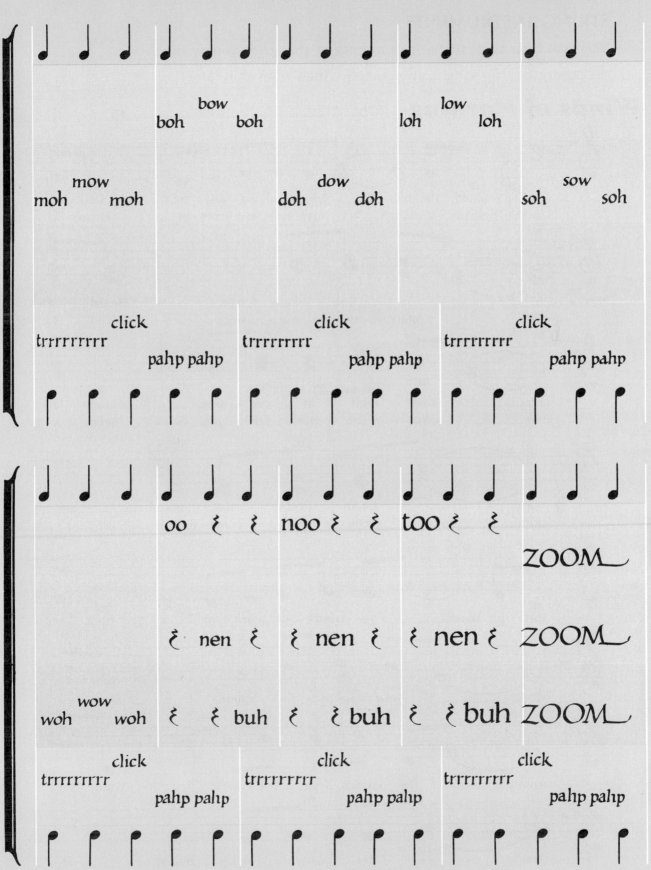

STRING INSTRUMENTS

You will hear two of the instruments of the string family on the recording of this song. Can you tell which ones they are?

Winds of Morning

WORDS AND MUSIC BY TOMMY MAKEM
COPYRIGHT © 1968 TOMMY MAKEM. USED BY PERMISSION OF TIN WHISTLE MUSIC, INC.

1. I've walked the hills_____ when rain was fall - ing,_____ Rest - ed
2. I've helped a plough - man tend his hors - es,_____ Heard a

by a white oak tree, Heard a
rip - pling riv - er sing, Talked to

lark_____ sing high at eve - ning,_____ Caught a
stars_____ when night was fall - ing,_____ Seen a

moon - beam on the sea._____
prim - rose wel - come spring._____

REFRAIN

Soft - ly blow,_____ ye winds of morn - ing; Sing, ye

winds,_____ your mourn - ful sound. Blow ye

from_____ the earth's four cor - ners;_____ Guide this

trav - - 'ler where he's bound.

3. By foreign shores my feet have wandered,
   Heard a stranger call me friend;
   Every time my mind was troubled,
   Found a smile around the bend.
   Refrain

4. There's a ship stands in the harbor,
   All prepared to cross the foam;
   Far off hills were fair and friendly,
   Still there's fairer hills at home.
   Refrain

For a cello part, play open strings D, C, and G, as indicated by the letters in the score.

For thicker density, add Autoharp or guitar, using chords D, A₇, and G. For guitar fingerings, see p. 204.

Listen for the higher sounds of the violins and violas, and the lower sounds of the cellos and string basses in this piece.

Tchaikowsky: *Serenade for Strings in C, "Waltz"*

BRASS INSTRUMENTS

Which instrument of the brass family is playing the melody of this song?

Christmas Is Coming
ENGLISH MELODY

1. Christ - mas is com - ing! The goose is get - ting fat!
2. If you've no pen - ny, A ha' - pen - ny will do,

Please to put a pen - ny in an old man's ___ hat,
If you have no ha' - pen - ny, Then God bless ___ you,

Please to put a pen - ny in an old man's hat.
If you have no ha' - pen - ny, Then God bless you.

These parts for trumpet and trombones can be added to the tone color of the voices.

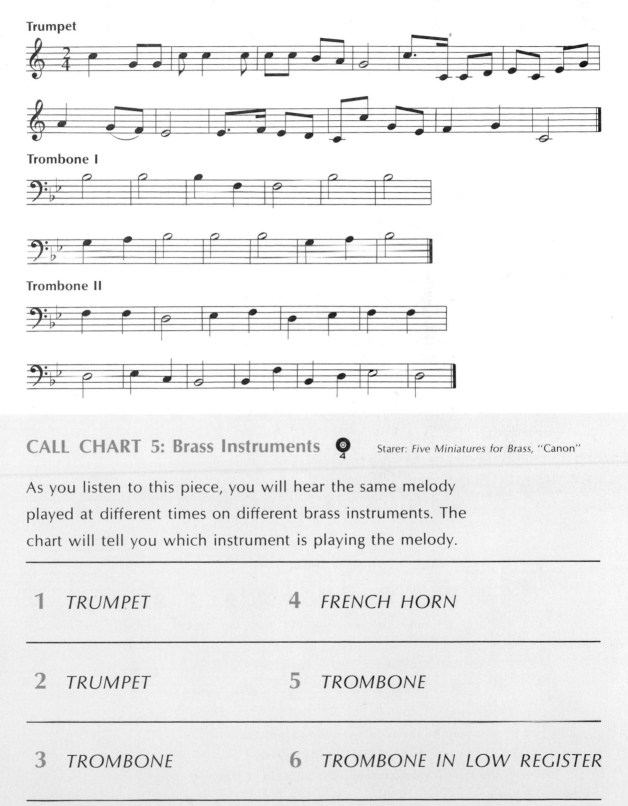

Trumpet

Trombone I

Trombone II

CALL CHART 5: Brass Instruments

Starer: *Five Miniatures for Brass, "Canon"*

As you listen to this piece, you will hear the same melody played at different times on different brass instruments. The chart will tell you which instrument is playing the melody.

1	*TRUMPET*	4	*FRENCH HORN*
2	*TRUMPET*	5	*TROMBONE*
3	*TROMBONE*	6	*TROMBONE IN LOW REGISTER*

WOODWIND INSTRUMENTS

Two instruments of the woodwind family are used on the recording of this song. Can you tell which ones they are?

Rain, Rain, Go Away

WORDS AND MUSIC BY FRED STARK AND JERRY VANCE

© 1973 POPDRAW MUSIC CORP.. USED BY PERMISSION

1. I'm watching the clock on the wall counting the minutes away,
   I can't wait to go spend the day with my friends.
   Time goes so slow, don't you know when the rain's pouring down,
   It's raining all over the ground, so I say:

REFRAIN

Rain, rain, go a-way,___ Hey, don't you know it's Sat-ur-day,___ The time I get to spend the day___ with my friends. Rain, rain, you bring me down.___ Noth-ing to do when you're all a-round___

Ending for verse 1.
But sit and lis-ten to the tick-ing sound___ of the clock.

Ending for verse 2.
tick-ing sound___ of the clock.

2. Alone in my room by myself playing the record machine,
   And looking for sunshine between all the clouds.
   Where is the sun? It's no fun when the blue sky is gray.
   I sure hope that Sunday will stay a sun day. *Refrain*

FOR WOODWIND PLAYERS

• Flutes and recorders can play the melody or harmony part in the refrain.

• Clarinets can play the part below to accompany the singing of the refrain.

Clarinet

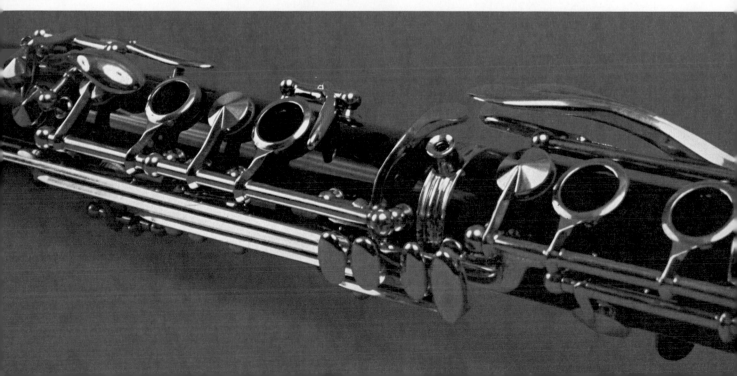

CALL CHART 6: Tone Color

In this Call Chart, you will hear the tone color of each of the woodwind instruments pictured. You will also hear a woodwind ensemble.

As each number is called, look at the pictures and listen to the sound.

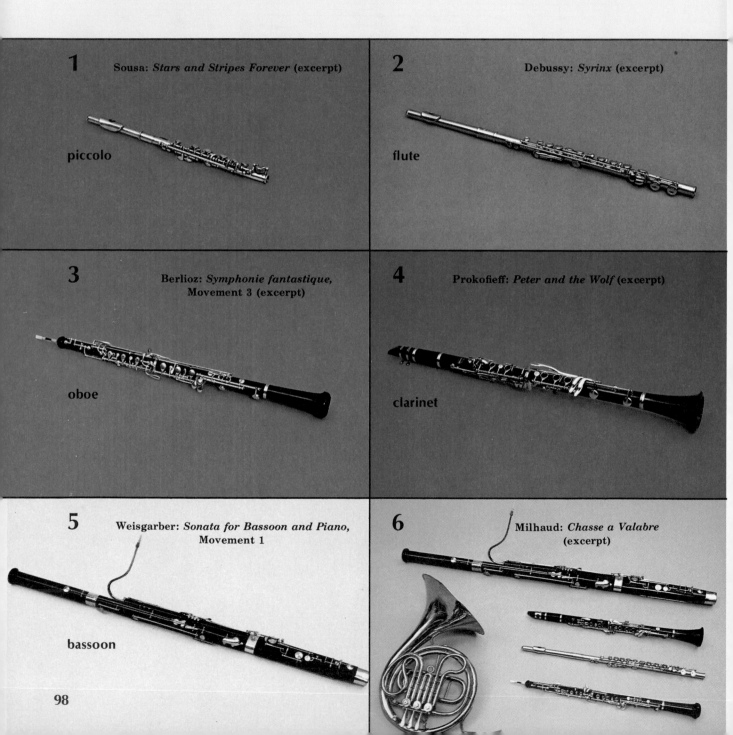

1 Sousa: *Stars and Stripes Forever* (excerpt)

piccolo

2 Debussy: *Syrinx* (excerpt)

flute

3 Berlioz: *Symphonie fantastique,* Movement 3 (excerpt)

oboe

4 Prokofieff: *Peter and the Wolf* (excerpt)

clarinet

5 Weisgarber: *Sonata for Bassoon and Piano,* Movement 1

bassoon

6 Milhaud: *Chasse a Valabre* (excerpt)

WHAT DO YOU HEAR? 4: Tone Color 🎵
5

These are tone colors you have heard or played. Do you hear one instrument, or a combination? On each line, circle what you hear.

1 VIOLIN   VIOLA   CELLO   STRING BASS   COMBINATION

2 GUITAR   AUTOHARP   RECORDER   COMBINATION

3 FLUTE   OBOE   CLARINET   BASSOON   COMBINATION

4 TRUMPET   TROMBONE   FRENCH HORN   COMBINATION

5 VIOLIN   VIOLA   CELLO   STRING BASS   COMBINATION

6 CHILDREN'S   MEN'S   WOMEN'S   COMBINATION
  VOICES   VOICES VOICES

7 GUITAR   AUTOHARP   RECORDER   COMBINATION

8 MARACAS   CLAVES   DRUMS   GUIRO   COMBINATION

9 TRUMPET   TROMBONE   FRENCH HORN   COMBINATION

10 FLUTE   OBOE   CLARINET   BASSOON   COMBINATION

Style: New Music

NEW SOUNDS

Composers have always been fascinated by new possibilities for sounds—new ways to produce them and new ways to put them together.

Composers might use traditional instruments in unusual ways . . . invent new instruments . . . create new sounds on an electronic sound instrument . . . or change sounds with tape recorders.

NEW SOUNDS FOR INSTRUMENTS AND VOICES

In this piece you will hear traditional instruments—strings, brass, woodwinds, percussion—used in some new ways. Can you discover some of the ways? Erb: *The Seventh Trumpet*

If you play an instrument used in that piece, experiment to find ways to make unusual sounds.

Voices can be used in unusual ways too. How many ways can you think of to make mouth sounds? Here are some. Try to think of others.

whispers	tongue clicks	lip-pops
shouts	moans	glides up and down

Can you create a piece using mouth and voice sounds? You might use a poem as part of it. You might build a score of the piece, such as:

poem with   lip-pops,   poem with

  moans,   tongue clicks SHOUTS silence SHOUTS   moans,

  whispers   (loud)   whispers

  (soft)   (getting soft)

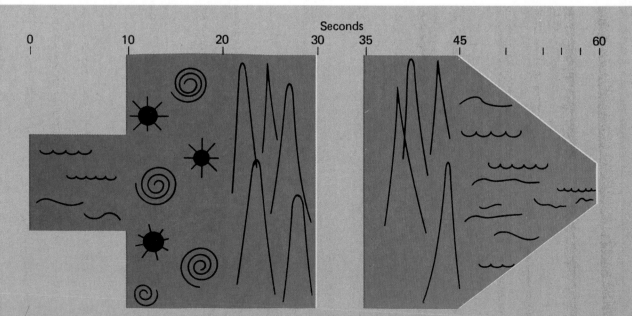

Another way to create new sounds with instruments or the voice is by amplification. A microphone can be placed in front of or directly on the sound maker. Connected to amplifiers that make the sound louder, the result is often an interesting new way to hear that instrument.

USING TAPE RECORDERS

In this piece for jazz band you will hear sounds electrically amplified. How many of these instruments can you hear?

flute   clarinet   oboe   bassoon
strings   piano   drums

🎵
5   Withers: *Lean On Me*

You can make some interesting sounds if you have a microphone and speakers. Attach the microphone to various instruments and try making unusual sounds. Put the microphone on your throat. Try making different voice sounds and see what happens.

You can make an amplified sound piece, with a score such as the one on p. 102. Try tape-recording your piece to play for others, asking them to guess how the sounds were made.

INVENTING NEW INSTRUMENTS

As composers look for new ways to make sounds, they sometimes invent new instruments.

Composer Harry Partch was not satisfied with just 12 tones within the octave, nor with the instruments that are built to play the 12 tones.

He invented his own instruments on which he could play 43 different tones within one octave. A picture of one of Mr. Partch's inventions—the cloud chamber bowls—is shown below.

Listen to a piece he composed for the cloud chamber bowls—large, 12-gallon glass bottles sawed in half. Each half is hung from a wire and struck with small, soft mallets.

🔘
5   Partch: *Cloud Chamber Music*

When you listen again, hear what makes the contrast in the second section.

1. strong, steady beat

2. melody played in several registers

3. contrast of tone color

4. use of singing voice

📖 Another composer of new music is featured in What People Do with Music-Compose, p. 124.

105

MAKE YOUR OWN INSTRUMENT

Try inventing instruments out of a variety of materials: tin cans, glasses, bottles, pot lids, etc.

Work in small groups to put together sounds. Try to get a musical result. Think of ways to notate your piece for others to play.

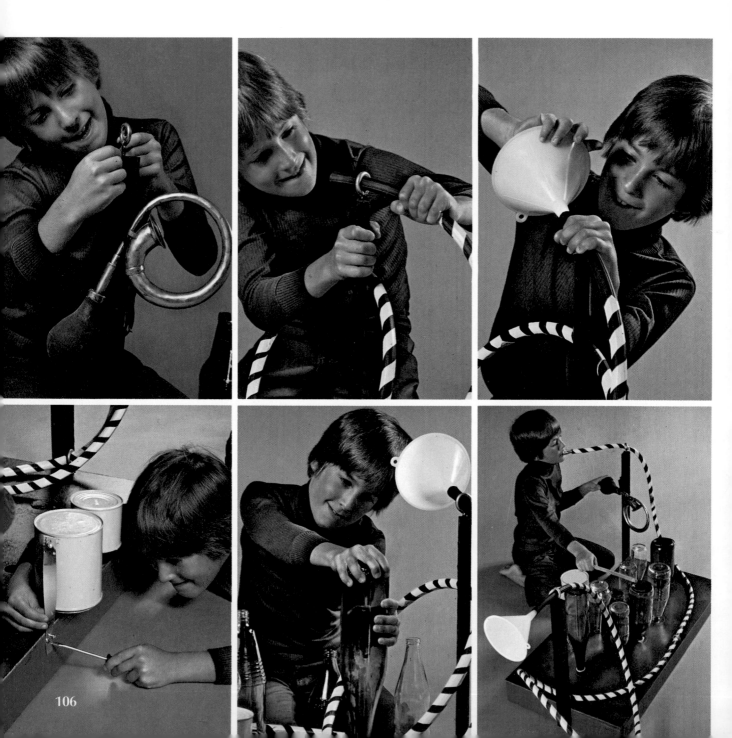

CREATING NEW VOICE SOUNDS

Use the tone color of your voice to recite this poem.

NIGHT SOUNDS

Night sounds
Depending where
Are very different
Loud and soft but never complete
Silence

David S. Walker

Now say the poem in a different way, adding one of the tone colors shown below.

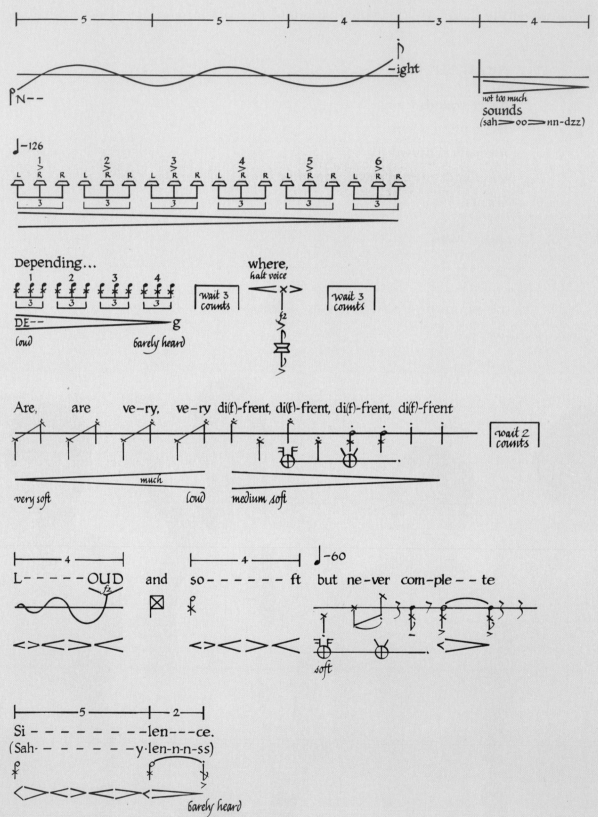

To perform this sound piece, follow the explanation of the
symbols in the legend. Use the recording to help you.

LEGEND

|———— seconds ————|

⟐L ⟐R left and right hands striking lap or thighs

⬡ both hands clapped

⫥ both hands cupped over mouth

⫰ both hands open around mouth

| unvoiced; only certain consonants will sound

⊠ normal speaking voice

**Listen to how one composer uses voices
in unusual ways to imitate frogs, toads,
insects, screech owls, and
the murmur of a breeze.**

● Ravel: *L'Enfant et les Sortilèges*,
"Andante," excerpt

Experiencing the Arts: Ornamentation

An *ornament* is a decoration added to "dress up" something. Can you find some things in the room that are "dressed up," or embellished, or decorated?

Can you find some things that do not use decorations—things that are not "dressed up"? Some things have ornamentation and some do not.

Look at these pictures and those on pages 112 and 113. Can you describe the ornaments used—or their lack of use—in each pair?

PLAIN AND FANCY

CHINESE SCULPTURE. SINGLE FIGURE OF MAITREYA. THE METROPOLITAN MUSEUM OF ART. KENNEDY FUND. 1926.

CHINESE SCULPTURE. MAITREYA ALTARPIECE. THE METROPOLITAN MUSEUM OF ART. ROGERS FUND. 1938.

DRESSING UP A MELODY

A melody can be ornamented too, by adding extra tones to "dress it up." If you know the melody and listen for it, you can better appreciate the ornaments added to it.

Here is a melody for you to sing. Learn it so you can sing it from memory.

Amazing Grace EARLY AMERICAN MELODY   WORDS BY JOHN NEWTON

1. A - maz - ing____ grace, how sweet the sound
2. The Lord has____ prom - ised good to me,

That saved a____ wretch like me!____
His word my____ hope se - cures;____

I once____ was____ lost, but now____ am____ found,
He will____ my____ shield and por - tion____ be

Was blind, but____ now I see.____
As long as____ life en - dures.____

The melody of "Amazing Grace" can be ornamented by adding extra tones to it. One way to add extra tones is to fill in some or all the tones between two melody notes

The____ Lord

or leave the melody note and return to it.

pro - mised

114

Here is an example of how a gospel singer ornaments the melody of "Amazing Grace." Listen to it and follow the words and the music. Half notes (♩) are used on the same syllables as in the original melody to help you keep your place.

Amazing Grace, ornamented version

2. The ___ Lord, the ___ Lord, ___

The ___ Lord has ___ prom - ised, promised good ___ to ___

me, ___ His ___ word my ___ hope ___ se - cures; ___ He ___

will _____ my shield _____ and ___

por - tion, por-tion be ___ As ___ long, ___

as long, ___ as ___ long ___ as ___ life _____

life _____ en - dures. _____

More About Tone Color

GAMELAN ORCHESTRA OF INDONESIA

Gamelans are orchestras in Indonesia composed of percussion, string, and wind instruments.

🎵 Hudan Mas (Golden Rain)

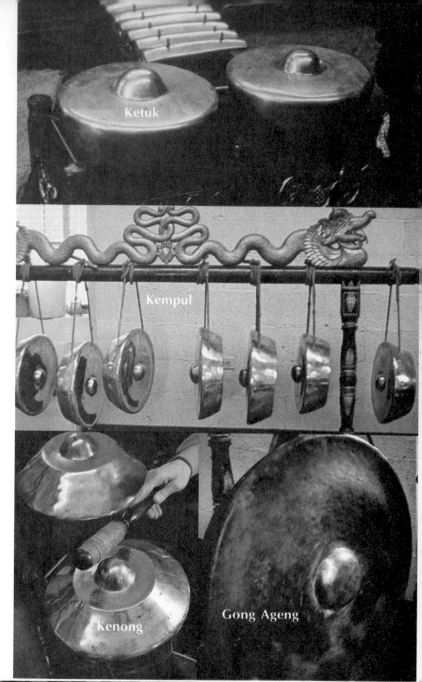

A SHORT PIECE FOR GAMELAN

Learn to play a short piece of gamelan music. Play the following phrases on bells, glockenspiels, or metallophones. Notice that each phrase repeats. As you play, keep the rhythm steady.

F   A   B♭   A   B♭   A   C   B♭

F   E   F   E   F   E   C   B♭

Other players add the tone color of a variety of gongs played on certain beats of the melody phrase. The gongs are pictured on p. 116.

Beats	1	2	3	4	5	6	7	8
Gong Ageng								x
Kenong		x		x		x		x
Kempul			x		x		x	
Ketuk	x	x	x	x	x	x	x	

These gongs can be made from kitchen pots and pans and the lids. Experiment with different ways to strike them.

Put all the parts together—melody played on glockenspiels or bells, accompanied by the gongs.

IPU AND PUILI STICKS OF HAWAII

In Hawaii, some instruments are made from gourds and bamboo. The *ipu* is a large hollow gourd that is struck with the heel of the hand and the tips of the fingers. Play this pattern on the ipu.

♩ = play with tips of fingers

♩ = play with heel of hand

Nani Wale Na Hala FOLK SONG FROM HAWAII

ENGLISH VERSION BY ALICE FIRGAU

For guitar fingerings, see p. 204.

Na - ni wa - le na ha - la, E - a, e - a.
Ke____ on - i a e - la,

O Na - u - e i - ke ka - i, E - a, e - a.
Pi - li ma - i Ha - e - na,

Lovely are the hala trees, Ea, ea.   *Near Haena halas grow, Ea, ea.*
Swaying by the gentle seas, Ea, ea.   *In Naue breezes blow, Ea, ea.*

The tapping of *puili* sticks adds a special tone color to that of the ipu. A puili stick is a piece of bamboo that is fringed on one end to make the stick flexible.

VERSE 1:				
Phrase 1: Tap sticks in front.	Tap sticks on floor to side.	Tap sticks in front.	Tap sticks on floor.	Repeat.
Phrase 2: Tap sticks overhead.	Tap right shoulder with right stick.	Tap sticks overhead.	Tap left shoulder with left stick.	Repeat.
VERSE 2:				
Phrase 1: Tap crossed sticks overhead from left to right.				Repeat from right to left.
Phrase 2: Tap sticks overhead.	Tap right shoulder with right stick.	Tap sticks overhead.	Tap left shoulder with left stick.	Repeat.

KOTO OF JAPAN

The koto is one of the most popular musical instruments in Japan. On this recording you will hear a koto playing an accompaniment for the well-known song, "Sakura." For a dance, see p. 250.

Sakura

FOLK SONG FROM JAPAN   MODERN ARRANGEMENT BY HENRY BURNETT   ENGLISH VERSION BY LORENE HOYT

5

1. Sa - ku - ra,   Sa - ku - ra,   Cher - ry blos - soms
2. Sa - ku - ra,   Sa - ku - ra,   Blos - soms wav - ing
   Sa - ku - ra,   Sa - ku - ra,   Ya - yo - i no

ev - 'ry - where. Clouds of glo - ry fill the ___ sky,
in the ___ breeze. Yo - shi - no, the cher - ry ___ land,
so - ra ___ wa, Mi - wa - ta - su ka - gi - ri,

Mist of beau - ty in the ___ air, Love - ly col - ors float - ing ___ by,
Tat - su - ta, the ma - ple ___ trees, Ka - ra - sa - ki, pine tree ___ grand,
Ka - su - mi ka ku - mo ka, Ni - o - i zo i - zu - ru;

Sa - ku - ra, Sa - ku - ra, Let ___ all come ___ sing - ing.
Sa - ku - ra, Sa - ku - ra, Let ___ all come ___ sing - ing.
I - za - ya, i - za - ya Mi ___ ni yu - kan. ___

Listen how the "Sakura" melody is used in a concert piece for koto. First you will hear the theme (the melody). Then you will hear three variations on the theme.

5 Eto: Variations on Sakura

Style: Eskimo and American Indian Song

When Christopher Columbus arrived in America, he was already a latecomer—the Indians and the Eskimos had been living here for thousands of years.

Television and movies usually give us just one view of the American Indian—that of the Plains Indian with his feathered bonnets, horses, tepees, buffalo hunting, and warfare.

However, the way of life of the Indian and the Eskimo showed much variety. Some were wandering hunters; others settled in villages and grew crops. Some were warlike; others were peaceful. Some groups had kings; others had headmen. Some were guided in their religious lives by priests; others had guardian spirits.

The music of the Indians and the Eskimos also showed much variety. Three different kinds of Indian music are from places pictured on the map.

Within each of these areas, the music is somewhat alike, but from one area to another it can be very different.

THE ESKIMO

The way of life and languages of the Eskimo are quite different
from Indians. The Eskimos live all across the top of the
North American continent. They survive in the very harsh climate
of the far north by hunting and by fishing. They adapt to their climate
through clever inventions like the igloo and the kayak.

The Eskimo's most important musical instrument is a large, shallow
tambourine drum covered with caribou skin.

Other instruments such as rattles, flutes, and whistles
are sometimes found, but by far the most important form of music
is the song accompanied by the drum.

As you listen to this Eskimo song about a musk ox hunt,
answer these questions.   *Musk Ox Hunt Song*

1. Is the range of pitches narrow, or wide?
2. Is the tempo slow, or fast?
3. How would you describe the tone color of the voices?

Other Eskimo songs often
comment on the problems
of life, including how hard
it is to make up songs!

THE NAVAJO

The Navajo Indians live on a reservation that lies in parts of Arizona, New Mexico, and Utah. They raise sheep and grow crops and are widely known for their weaving and their silverwork.

This song is part of the Night Chant, or Yeibichei, an important nine-day ceremony in which boys and girls are initiated into the religious life of the tribe.

Listen to discover how the voices in this song are different from the Eskimo song. 🔘 *Night Chant Song*

When you listen again, answer some other questions.

1. What instrument accompanies the voices?

2. Is the beat steady?

3. What is the tempo?

4. Is the range of pitches wide, or narrow?

5. Does the melody focus on one important tone?

All of these qualities make up a style that is very different from that of the Eskimos.

THE SALISH

In western Montana, between the Navajos and the Eskimos, live the Salish Indians. Their music and dance, often centered traditionally on ideas of war, are clearly in the style of Plains Indians.

The kind of music the Salish sang—and still sing—in their *War Dance Song* is the same type sung by other Plains Indians such as the Sioux, Cheyenne, Arapaho, and Blackfeet. It is also the kind of music we usually hear on television or in the movies when Indians are shown.

Listen to a *War Dance Song* sung by a mixed group of Salish and Blackfeet Indians. What are some of the things you hear?

🔘 *War Dance Song*
6

Not all Eskimo music sounds like the *Musk Ox Hunt Song,* or all Navajo music like the *Night Chant,* or all Salish music like the *War Dance Song.* Much variety exists in the music of each of these societies.

THE CHANGING SCENE

The music of all these groups is changing. What you have heard is traditional song, but the Indians and Eskimos of today sing and play other types of music—guitar songs, rock, jazz, country-Western, classical, and all the other kinds of music found in the United States.

Music always changes, and music in Indian and Eskimo societies is changing too.

Careers in Music: Compose

Many composers today use traditional instruments in unusual ways, or they find or invent sound sources. On the recording, Donald Erb tells how he composes.

You will hear *Trio for Two* and a piece he composed for you, *Nightmusic for Nine*.

 What People Do with Music: Compose

6

SOUND PIECE 4: Nightmusic for Nine

Donald Erb

Scored for:

1. Autoharp or piano (One player); Mark end of strings with colored tape for easy identification.

2. Harmonica in C. Cover all the E's with small strips of masking tape.

3. Five 10 oz. pop bottles partially filled with water, to be tuned as shown and placed in order from left to right. (Five players)

4. Maracas (One player); Slide whistle (One player).

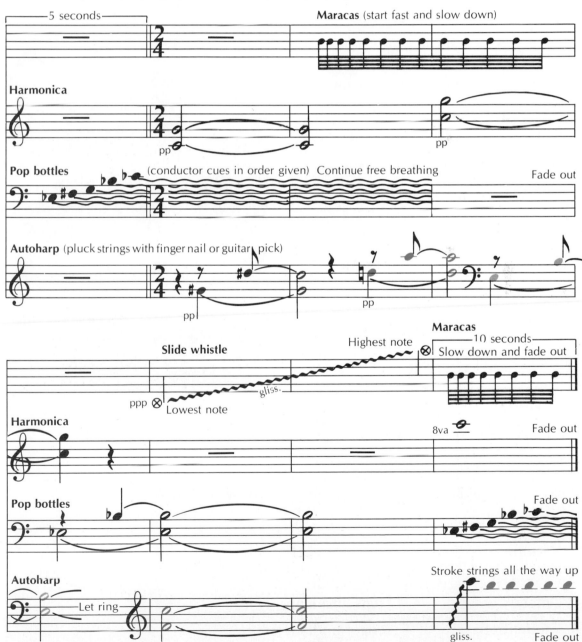

Using What You Know About Melody, Harmony, and Texture

Glance very quickly at this painting. Look up as soon as you recognize what it is. What did you see?

Now look at the painting again, but this time very carefully and slowly. Notice as many details about it as you can. Think about how the painting uses these qualities:

colors	lines
shapes	directions
repetitions	depth
contrasts	distortion

Now listen to a piece of music. As it is playing, read pages 126 and 127. Try to get as much from your reading as you can.

🎧 Haydn: *Symphony 45,* Movement 3 (excerpt)

Now listen again. *Listen hard.* Try to hear how the music uses these qualities:

tempo	contrasts
beat	tone colors
meter	steps and leaps
repetitions	longer and shorter notes

On the following pages you will learn more about three qualities of music—*melody, harmony,* and *texture.*

Melody is the way single tones are played, one after the other. We can picture melody with a line that shows its contour.

Harmony is the way tones are sounded together, usually chords that accompany a melody.

Two or more melodies can be played at the same time.

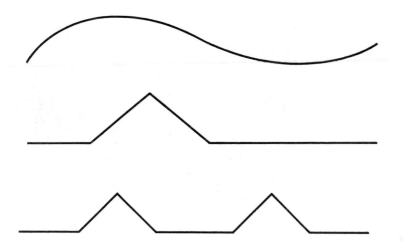

Texture is the way melodies and harmonies work together.

Works of art want to make us look "hard," listen "hard," and think "hard." It takes some work to enjoy art. Thinking more lets us feel more.

FOLLOW THE CONTOUR

This song has four phrases. The line below shows the shape, or contour, made by the notes in the first phrase.

As you listen to the recording, follow the contour of the melody in each phrase. Can you find another phrase that has the same contour as phrase 1?

The Music Is You

WORDS AND MUSIC BY JOHN DENVER

Sing the song as a two-part round to hear the texture of two lines of melody working together.

STEPS, LEAPS, REPEATS

The tones of a melody can repeat; they can move upward or downward by step or by leap. The way the tones move gives the melody a shape, or contour. Take turns singing the echo parts in this folk song from Greece and notice how the tones move.

The Ocean Waves

FOLK SONG FROM GREECE   ENGLISH WORDS BY MARIA JORDAN

1. The o - cean waves, the o - cean waves are az - ure blue._____ Their rock - ing
2. The o - cean waves, the o - cean waves, they splash their dew._____ And drops fall

mo - tion lul - la - bies my love to sleep._____ She slum - bers in my
ev - 'ry - where no mat - ter what you do._____ Rock gent - ly 'gainst my

fish - ing boat. Be still, or she may wak - en._____
lit - tle boat. A spe - cial some - one's sleep - ing!_____

(Waves come and go)   (all day and night)
Waves come and go_____ all day and night. _____ Waves come and

(echo each time)
go _____ through dark and light._____ The tide comes in,_____ the tide moves

out._____ A won - drous thing _____ with - out a doubt.

📖 For another song from Greece, see p. 244.
📖 For a percussion part, see p. 233.

129

SAME WORDS, DIFFERENT MELODIES

Scarborough Fair

FOLK SONG FROM ENGLAND

VERSION ONE

1. Are you go - ing to Scar - bor - ough fair,
2. Tell her to make me a cam - bric shirt,
3. Tell her to wash it in yon - der well,

Pars - ley, sage, rose-ma - ry, and thyme; With - out any seam — or
Re - mem - ber me — to
Where never spring wa - ter nor

one who lives there,
nee - dle work, For once she was a true love of mine.
rain ev - er fell,

Sometimes a folk singer has to choose between different versions of the same song. Here is an English ballad sung two ways. Listen to the two versions and choose one to sing.

Although the story remains the same, the music sounds different.

130

Scarborough Fair

FOLK SONG FROM ENGLAND

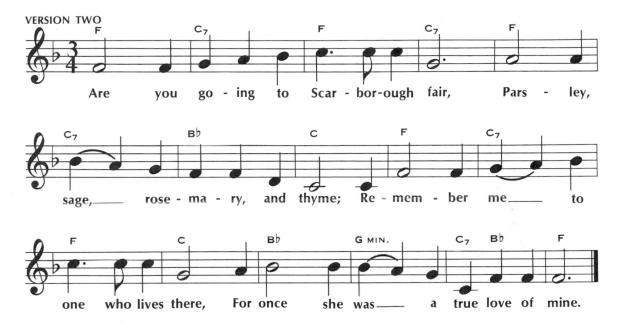

Compare the two versions of "Scarborough Fair" by answering the questions below.

VERSION TWO

Are you go - ing to Scar - bor-ough fair, Pars - ley, sage,____ rose - ma - ry, and thyme; Re - mem - ber me____ to one who lives there, For once she was____ a true love of mine.

WHAT MAKES THE DIFFERENCE?

1. How many phrases are there in each version?

2. In which version do you find two phrases that are alike?

3. Which version is major? Which is minor?

4. What is the meter of each version?

These are some things to look for when you are trying to find out how a melody works: phrases, repetitions, contrasts, major and minor, meter.

Try analyzing other melodies in your book including the chorus and recorder satellites.

SOUND PIECE 5: Register

Walkin' Talkin' Blues Doris Hays 6

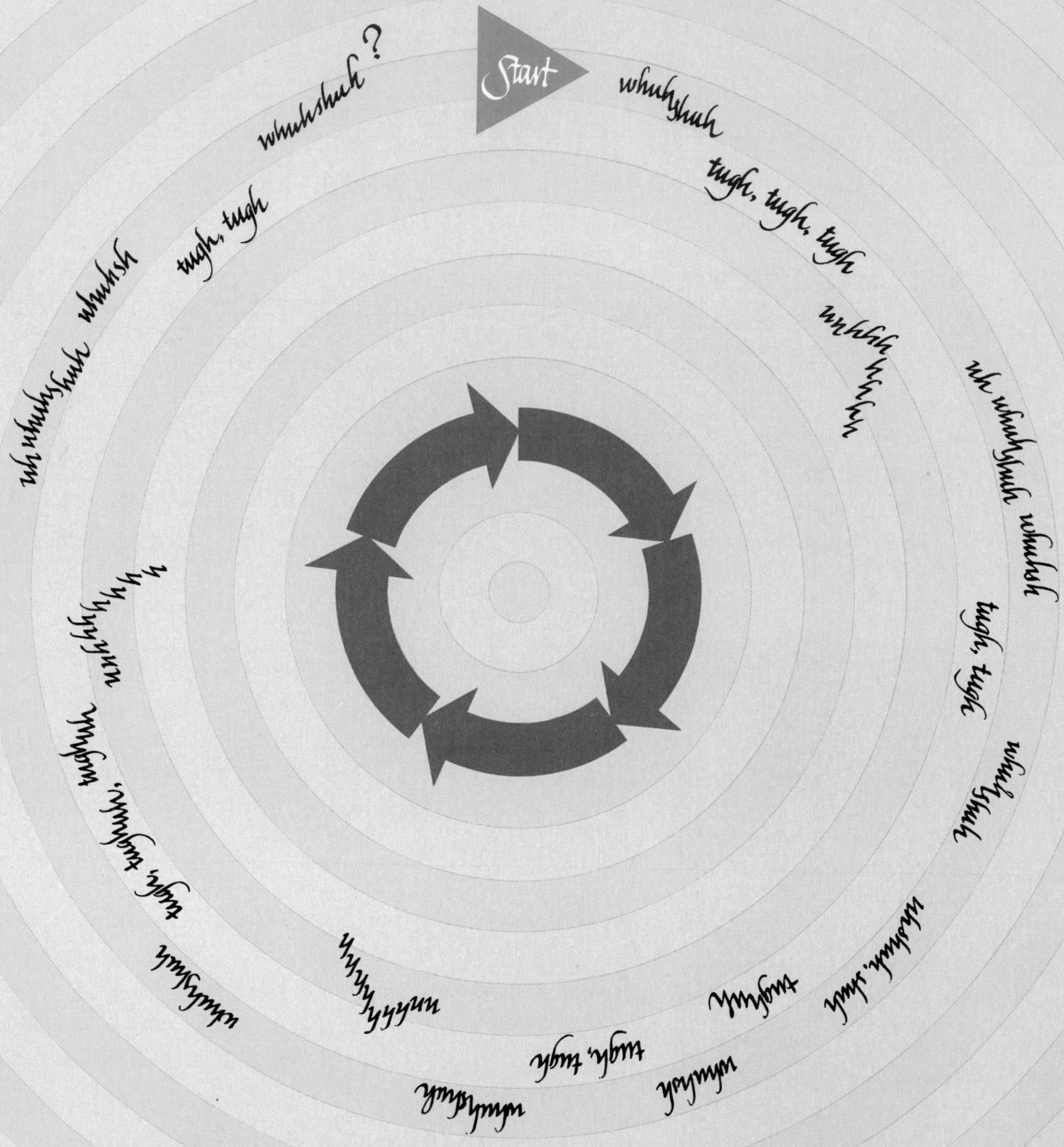

REGISTER: HIGH, LOW

Some parts for keyboard are played in a high register and some
in a low register.

If you play the piano, practice the high part, called *Primo,* in
this duet. Ask someone to play the low part, called *Secondo,*
with you.

Russian Folk Song Peter Ilyitch Tchaikowsky

REGISTER: HIGH, MIDDLE, LOW

Choose one of the phrases in this song to play on the piano.
Use high, middle, or low register as shown by the keyboard
diagram.

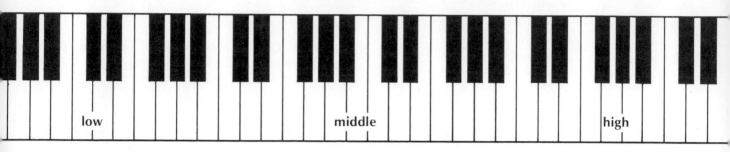

low   middle   high

Everybody Loves Saturday Night
FOLK SONG FROM GHANA

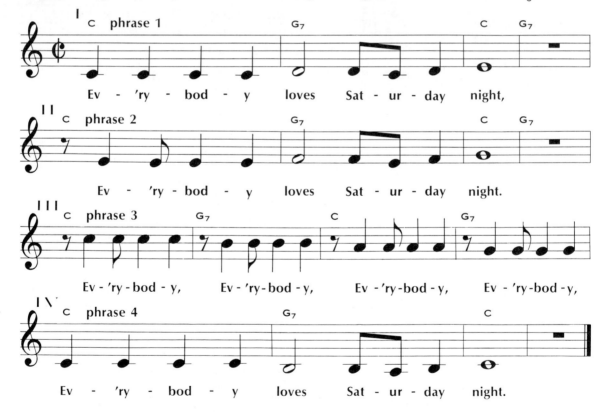

Ask three friends to play other phrases with you. Play them one
after the other. Then play any two phrases together, then three,
then four. The melody can also be played as a round.

Another time, try playing the steady beat in the lowest register.
Play low C four times, and low G four times throughout the song.

     For guitar fingerings, see p. 204.

In this piece for organ you will hear a melody, called a *subject*, played in different registers. It is woven together with countermelodies as the music moves along. This piece is written in a special form called *fugue*.

The chart will help you hear the melody moving from one register to another.

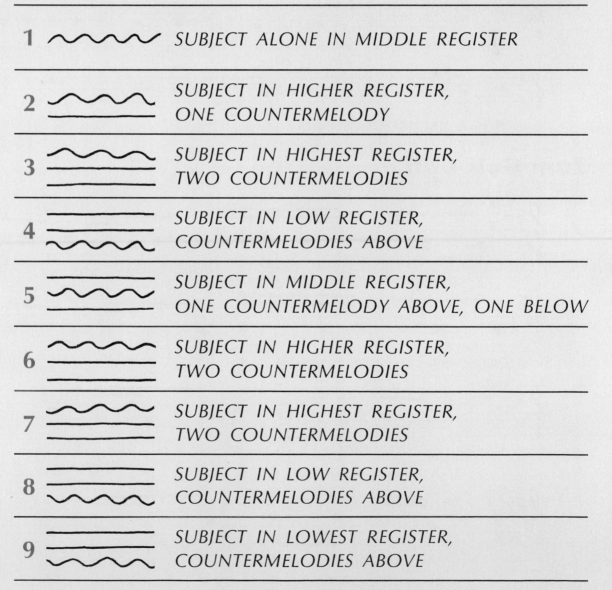

1	〰️	*SUBJECT ALONE IN MIDDLE REGISTER*
2		*SUBJECT IN HIGHER REGISTER, ONE COUNTERMELODY*
3		*SUBJECT IN HIGHEST REGISTER, TWO COUNTERMELODIES*
4		*SUBJECT IN LOW REGISTER, COUNTERMELODIES ABOVE*
5		*SUBJECT IN MIDDLE REGISTER, ONE COUNTERMELODY ABOVE, ONE BELOW*
6		*SUBJECT IN HIGHER REGISTER, TWO COUNTERMELODIES*
7		*SUBJECT IN HIGHEST REGISTER, TWO COUNTERMELODIES*
8		*SUBJECT IN LOW REGISTER, COUNTERMELODIES ABOVE*
9		*SUBJECT IN LOWEST REGISTER, COUNTERMELODIES ABOVE*

MELODY WITH CHORD ACCOMPANIMENT

A melody can be sung or played alone, or it can have a chord accompaniment. (Find the diagrams on p. 127 that show two kinds of texture—a melody alone, and a melody with chord accompaniment.) After singing the melodies of these two songs, add a chord accompaniment on piano or guitar. Each melody uses the E minor chord.

Hey, Ho! Nobody Home
OLD ENGLISH ROUND

E MIN.

Hey, ho! No - bo - dy home. Meat nor drink nor mon - ey have I none,

Yet I will be mer - ry.___ Hey, ho! No - bo - dy home.

Zum Gali Gali
FOLK SONG FROM ISRAEL

Ⓐ E MIN.

Zum ga - li ga - li, ga - li, Zum ga - li ga - li,

E MIN.   Fine

Zum ga - li ga - li, ga - li, Zum ga - li ga - li.

Ⓑ E MIN.

1. He - cha - lutz l' - man a - vo - dah;___
2. A - vo - dah l' - man he - cha - lutz;___

E MIN.   D.C. al Fine

___ A - vo - dah l' - man he - cha - lutz.
___ He - cha - lutz l' - man a - vo - dah.

  For directions for dancing the hora, see p. 243.

TWO MELODIES TOGETHER

Another way to vary the texture is to perform two melodies at the same time. (Find the diagram on p. 127 that shows two or more melodies played together.) Sing "Zum Gali Gali" again. This time, sing the melody of section A while others sing the melody of section B.

Now, listen to the recording of "Vine and Fig Tree." You will hear voices singing the melody while an oboe plays a countermelody. Then, when *you* can sing the melody, choose someone to play the countermelody on an instrument.

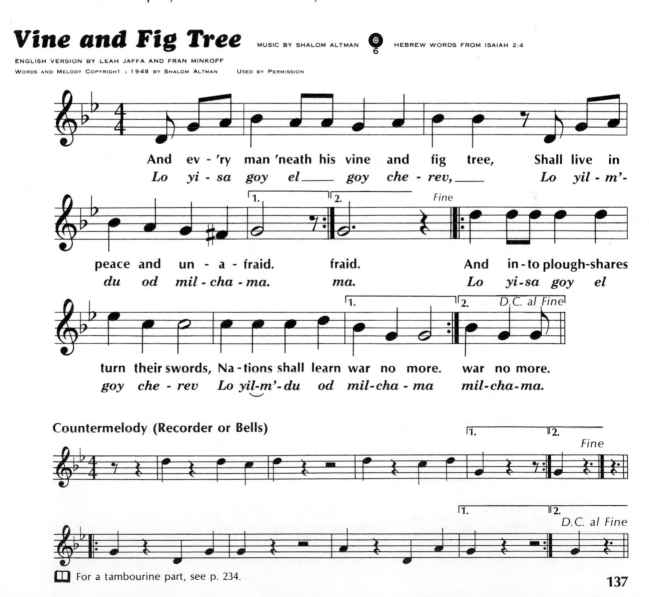

Vine and Fig Tree

MUSIC BY SHALOM ALTMAN   HEBREW WORDS FROM ISAIAH 2:4

ENGLISH VERSION BY LEAH JAFFA AND FRAN MINKOFF
WORDS AND MELODY COPYRIGHT © 1948 BY SHALOM ALTMAN   USED BY PERMISSION

And ev - 'ry man 'neath his vine and fig tree, Shall live in
Lo yi - sa goy el___ goy che - rev,___ Lo yil - m'-

1.   2.   Fine

peace and un - a - fraid.   fraid.   And in - to plough-shares
du od mil - cha - ma.   ma.   Lo yi - sa goy el

1.   2.   D.C. al Fine

turn their swords, Na - tions shall learn war no more.   war no more.
goy che - rev Lo yil-m'-du od mil-cha - ma   mil-cha-ma.

Countermelody (Recorder or Bells)

1.   2.   Fine

1.   2.   D.C. al Fine

For a tambourine part, see p. 234.

CHORDS AND COUNTERMELODY

Listen for the chords that accompany "You're My Friend" on the recording. And listen especially for the piano countermelody in verse 3.

Use an easy "lying-in-the-sun" voice when you sing this song.

You're My Friend

WORDS AND MUSIC BY CHRIS DEDRICK

'Cause you're my friend.___ You're my friend.___

You're my friend___ till the end, You're my friend.___

CODA (last time only)   *rit.*

You're my friend.___   You're my friend.___

2. Remember when I threw a snowball;
   Broke the Christmas light upon your tree?
   How your dad did yell, How I ran away,
   Why did you go tell him that you did it?
   You were punished 'stead of me.
   'Cause you're my friend. You're my friend.
   You're my friend till the end, You're my friend.

3. Hate to see you move away now.
   Listen to the sad call of the wren.
   Some ol' lucky guy will be your new-found friend,
   Love you just as I have—In my mind
   You'll be beside me till the end.
   'Cause you're my friend. You're my friend.
   You're my friend till the end, You're my friend.
   (*To Coda*)

When you know the song, add your own accompaniment by playing chords on the keyboard or bells. Play alone or with a friend.

Start with chord 1, which is played in every measure indicated by * in the score. Otherwise, play chord 2.

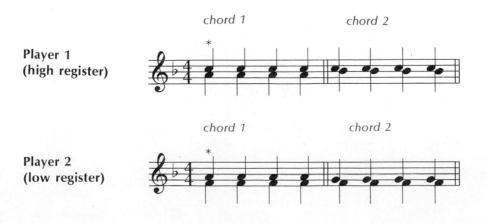

Player 1 (high register)

Player 2 (low register)

SOUND PIECE 6: Juncture Dance 1   **Doris Hays**

By Doris Hays © 1973 Tallapoosa Music

Look at the score of this sound piece to find the separate parts that move horizontally (side to side). When these parts are played together, they "fit" and support each other.

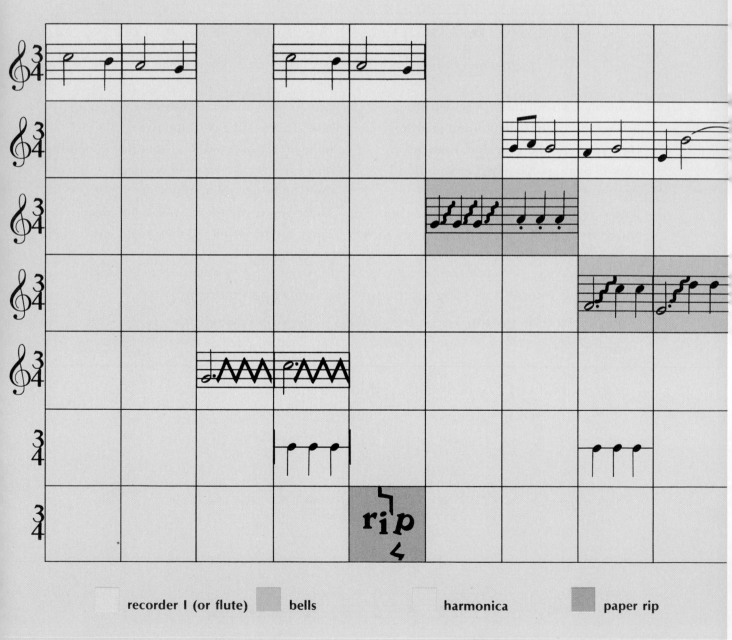

recorder I (or flute)   bells   harmonica   paper rip

For recorder fingerings, see p. 251.

Autoharp: ∿∿∿ means to strum. Let the strings sound for the full value of the note. Pluck the two quarter notes.

Harmonica: ∧∧∧ means to blow with a puffy sound, both in and out.

Paper rip: rip slowly so the sound lasts for three beats.
Memorize your part. Try other arrangements of the color blocks.

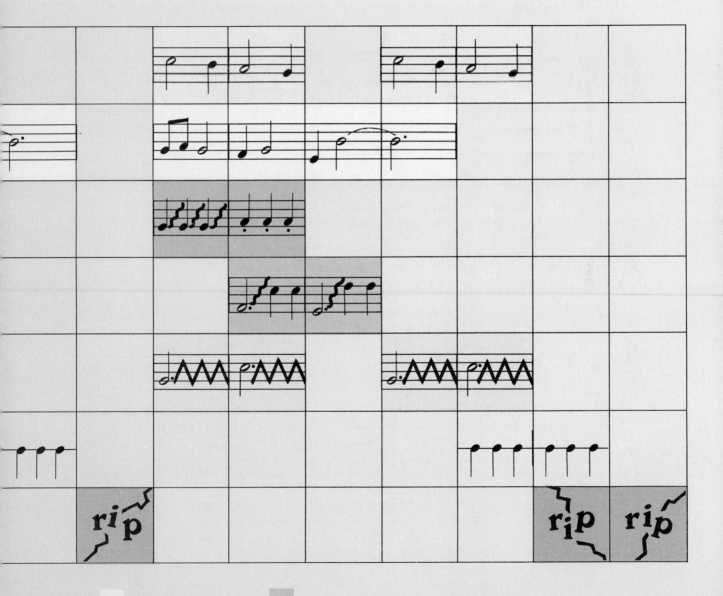

recorder II (or flute)   **Autoharp**   **triangle or claves**   © 1973 Doris Hays

LISTENING FOR DIFFERENT TEXTURES

Listen to the recording to hear how different textures are used.

- chord introduction
- melody performed as a round
- melody alone
- melody performed as a round
- melody with harmony and countermelody played by an oboe

Mee Y'Maleyl

HEBREW FOLK MELODY   ENGLISH VERSION BY JUDITH K. EISENSTEIN

FROM THE GATEWAY TO JEWISH SONG   © 1939 BY BEHRMAN'S JEWISH BOOK HOUSE, NEW YORK   USED BY PERMISSION

Mee y'-ma-leyl g'vu-rot Yis-ra-eyl? O - tan mee yim - neh?
Who can re-tell the things that be-fell us? Who can count them?

Heyn, b'-chal dor ya-kum ha-gib-bor Go-eyl ha - am.
In ev-'ry age a he - ro or sage came to our aid.

Sh'ma! Ba - ya - meem ha - heym ba - z'man ha - zeh,
Ah! At this time of year in days of yore,

Ma - ka - bee mo-shee - a u - fo - deh. Uv' - ya - mey - nu kal am Yis - ra -
Mac-ca-bees the tem-ple did re-store. And to-day our peo-ple, as we

eyl, Yit - a - hkheyd ya - kum l' - hig - ga - eyl.
dreamed, Will a - rise, u - nite, and be re - deemed.

Add a percussion accompaniment as others sing.

Tambourine   etc.

Drum   etc.

Christmas Canon

WORDS AND MUSIC BY DAVID EDDLEMAN

Play this bell part throughout "Christmas Canon" to create a different texture.

I See him slum - b'ring in ___ the hay, He's

II sleep - ing at the close of day. Come

III sing his praise ___ to God ___ on ___ high, But

IV sing soft - ly, sing.

Alleluia, Amen

TRADITIONAL ROUND

I Al - le - lu - ia, al - le - lu - ia.

II A - men, a - men.

Accompany the singing of "Alleluia, Amen" by playing this countermelody, called a *peal,* on the bells.

Style: Same Melody in Different Styles

In the graphic above, the letter G is printed in various ways. A melody can be performed in a variety of ways, too—by changing the rhythm, tempo, dynamics, tone color, and texture.

Follow the score as you listen to "Greensleeves" played as a melody alone.

Greensleeves
FOLK SONG FROM ENGLAND

The old year now a-way is fled, The new year it is

en-ter-ed, Then let us now our sins down tread And

joy-ful-ly all ap-pear. Let's mer-ry

be this day And let us now both sport and play.

Hang grief, cast care a-way, God send you a hap-py new year.

CALL CHART 8: Style 🎵 *Greensleeves*

Here is a sound collage using the same melody in different styles.
The chart will help you hear how texture and tone color are used.

What other differences can you hear in the various styles—in
rhythm, in tempo, in dynamics?

	TEXTURE	TONE COLOR
1	MELODY WITH ACCOMPANIMENT	GUITAR
2	MELODY WITH ACCOMPANIMENT	VOICES, ENGLISH HORN, GUITAR, FINGER CYMBALS
3	MELODY WITH ACCOMPANIMENT	STRINGS, HARP, FLUTE
4	MELODY ALONE	CARILLON (BELLS)
5	MELODY WITH ACCOMPANIMENT	VOICE, LUTE
6	MELODY WITH COUNTERMELODY	WOODWINDS

In addition to all the other ways *Greensleeves* has been used, it
has also been sung with different words. Which version will you sing?

Alas, my love, you do me wrong
To cast me off discourteously,
And I have loved you too long,
Delighting in your company.

Greensleeves is all my joy,
Greensleeves is my delight,
Greensleeves is my heart of gold
And who but my Lady Greensleeves?"

145

Careers in Music: Perform

Today's performer is likely to be equally familiar with recording studios and concert halls.

David Spinozza plays all styles from classical guitar to rock. On the recording, he tells some of the many ways he performs music.

7

For more about the guitar, see "Playing the Guitar," beginning on p. 189.

More About Melody, Harmony, and Texture

SEQUENCES—SAME PATTERN, DIFFERENT LEVELS

Follow the score as you listen to this song. Notice especially the melody patterns in the first three phrases of section B. How are they alike? How are they different?

Island Hopping

FOLK SONG FROM GREECE   ENGLISH WORDS BY MARIA JORDAN

1. Bags are packed and all is rea - dy, can't wait____ to
Boat is board-ing at the jet - ty, soon we'll____ de -

start; (can't wait____ to start;)
part; (soon we'll____ de - part;)

Is - land hop-ping we____ are____ go - ing,

Sea is calm, a soft____ wind's____ blow - ing,

We can feel ex - cite - ment____ grow - ing

in ev - 'ry heart,____ Ahs-toh kah loh____ In ev - 'ry____ heart.

When you know the song, try singing the harmony part.

CALL CHART 9: Sequences 🎯

How many things can you hear in the melody phrases of this Basque folk song? The symbol or word in the chart will tell you what happens in each phrase.

Begiak, Barres, Barres

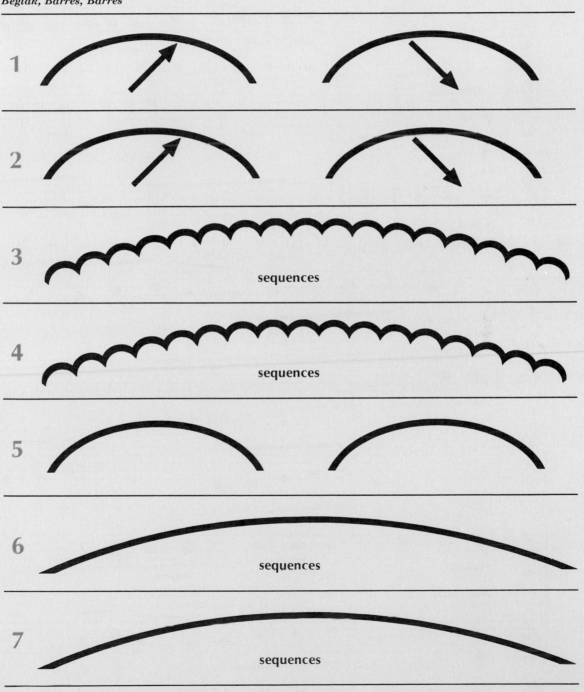

1

2

3   **sequences**

4   **sequences**

5

6   **sequences**

7   **sequences**

MORE ABOUT SEQUENCES

The words of this folk song from Africa mean "We are the
burning fire; we burn, we burn, we burn."

Tina Singu

FOLK SONG FROM AFRICA

FROM CHANSONS DE NOTRE CHALET.   COURTESY OF WORLD AROUND SONGS, BURNSVILLE, N.C.

Ti - na Sing - u, le - lu - vu - tae - o. Wat - sha,___ Wat - sha,___

Wat - sha. ___ Wat - sha,___ Wat - sha,___ Wat - sha,___ Wat - sha,___

Wat - sha. ___ La, la - la - la - la - la - la, la - la - la - la - la -

la, la - la - la - la - la - la - la - la - la - la - la.

Wat - sha, ___ Wat - sha, ___

La, la - la - la - la - la - la, la - la - la - la - la -

Wat - sha,___ Wat - sha,___ Wat - sha. ___

la, la - la - la - la - la - la - la - la - la - la.

WHAT DO YOU HEAR? 5: Sequences

Listen to the recording. Each time a number is called, decide whether you hear sequences. If you do, choose the word *sequences*. If you do not, choose the words *no sequences*.

---

1   SEQUENCES   NO SEQUENCES

Vivaldi: *Concerto in G Minor,* Movement 3

---

2   SEQUENCES   NO SEQUENCES

Dvořák: *Slavonic Dance No. 1*

---

3   SEQUENCES   NO SEQUENCES

Mouret: *Symphonie de fanfares,* "Rondeau"

---

4   SEQUENCES   NO SEQUENCES

"By the Waters of Babylon"

---

5   SEQUENCES   NO SEQUENCES

Vaughan Williams: *Fantasia on Greensleeves*

---

6   SEQUENCES   NO SEQUENCES

Scarlatti: *Sonata in D Minor*

INTERVALS—THE DISTANCE BETWEEN TONES

The hands of a clock measure how time moves in *intervals*. The intervals of time are called seconds, minutes, and hours.

Notes on a staff measure how tones move in intervals. The intervals of music can be called *steps, leaps,* and *repeats.*

Listen to the Westminster chimes as they measure quarter-hour intervals. Can you hear and see the intervals between the tones?

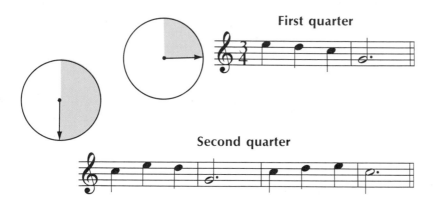

First quarter

Second quarter

Third quarter

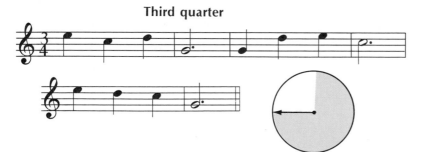

Fourth quarter

Now toll the hour, using a low-C bell. What interval will you hear—steps, leaps, or repeats?

152

OUTLINING A CHORD

Play an F chord by strumming the strings of an Autoharp very slowly. Listen to the different tones that make up an F chord—F, A, and C. Find a part of the melody of this song that outlines the F chord.

In the same way, listen to the tones of the C_7 chord—C, E, G, and B^b. Find a part of the melody that outlines the C_7 chord.

La Cucaracha

FOLK MELODY FROM MEXICO   WORDS BY RICHARD EISMAN

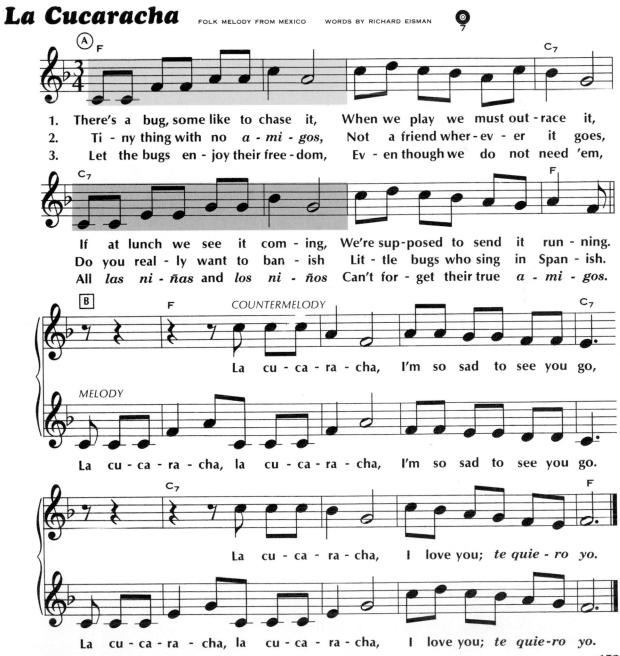

1. There's a bug, some like to chase it, When we play we must out-race it,
2. Ti - ny thing with no *a - mi - gos,* Not a friend wher-ev-er it goes,
3. Let the bugs en - joy their free - dom, Ev - en though we do not need 'em,

If at lunch we see it com - ing, We're sup-posed to send it run - ning.
Do you real - ly want to ban - ish Lit - tle bugs who sing in Span - ish.
All *las ni - ñas* and *los ni - ños* Can't for - get their true *a - mi - gos.*

COUNTERMELODY

La cu - ca - ra - cha, I'm so sad to see you go,

MELODY

La cu - ca - ra - cha, la cu - ca - ra - cha, I'm so sad to see you go.

La cu - ca - ra - cha, I love you; *te quie - ro yo.*

La cu - ca - ra - cha, la cu - ca - ra - cha, I love you; *te quie-ro yo.*

For a recorder ensemble, see p. 218. For a dance, see p. 246.

153

MELODIES THAT OUTLINE CHORDS

This melody is based on chords in the C family—C, G, and F.

Which chord is outlined in each color box?

Matilda FOLK SONG FROM JAMAICA

2. My money was to buy me house and land,
   The woman she got a serious plan.
   Matilda, she take me money and run Venezuela.
   Refrain

3. Now the money was safe in me bed,
   Stuck in the pillow beneath me head,
   But Matilda, she find me money and run Venezuela.
   Refrain

4. Never will I love again,
   All me money gone in vain
   'Cause Matilda, she take me money and run Venezuela.
   Refrain

For a percussion ensemble, see p. 235.

The Lord Is My Shepherd

BLACK SPIRITUAL

This melody is based on chords in the G family—G, D_7, and C.

In which two phrases does the melody outline the G chord?

1. The Lord,___ the Lord,___ the Lord is my shep-herd, The
2. He makes___ me lie down in green, green___ pas-tures, He

Lord, the Lord,___ the Lord is my shep-herd, The
makes me lie down in green, green___ pas-tures, He

Lord,___ the Lord,___ the Lord is my shep-herd, The
makes___ me lie down in green, green___ pas-tures,

Lord is my shep-herd and I shall not want.

3. He leads me beside the still, still waters, (*3 times*)
   The Lord is my shepherd and I shall not want.

4. I'll fear no evil for Thou art with me, (*3 times*)
   The Lord is my shepherd and I shall not want.

ON YOUR OWN

Find places in other songs where the melody outlines a chord.

- On Top of Old Smoky, p. 64
- Water Come a Me Eye, p. 84
- The Hammer Song, p. 86

For guitar fingerings, see p. 204.

THE CHROMATIC SCALE

The melodies you sing, play, and listen to are made up of arrangements of tones, some of which are a half step apart and others a whole step apart. To show half steps, line up all the bells from low C to high C.

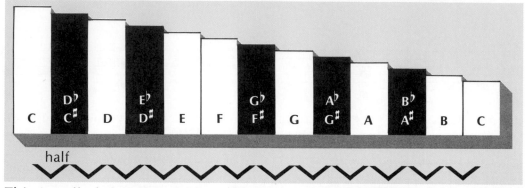

This is called the *chromatic scale*. To hear its general sound, play the bells upward, then downward. Play single tones and clusters of tones.

Here is a melody that is based on part of the chromatic scale.
Select the bells shown and try to play the melody with the recording while others sing.

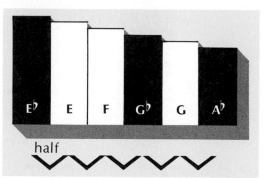

A Song with No Key

WORDS AND MUSIC BY DAVID EDDLEMAN

Not too fast   *mp*

How can there be a song with no key? It's hard to see how it can be. Lis - ten to me and you will a - gree_____ There is no key. Oh, me.

THE WHOLE-TONE SCALE

Using the whole chromatic scale, change the half steps to whole steps by removing every second bell.

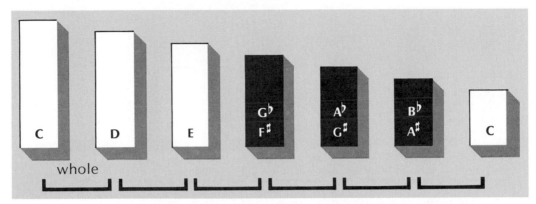

This is called the *whole-tone scale*. To hear the general sound, play the scale upward, then downward. Play single tones and clusters of tones.

This melody is based on a whole-tone scale. Sing or play it with the recording.

Silent Sea WORDS AND MUSIC BY DAVID EDDLEMAN

THE MAJOR SCALE

Many melodies you know are based on an arrangement of whole and half steps called a *major scale*.

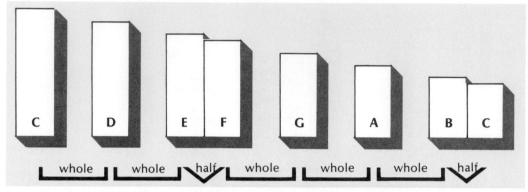

Play all the white keys or bells from low C to high C to hear the sound of the major scale in the key of C.

Now play "Jingle Bells" by ear, starting on E.

Practice building major scales in other keys: low D to high D, low F to high F, low G to high G, etc.

THE MINOR SCALE

Many melodies you know are based on another arrangement of whole and half steps called a *minor scale*.

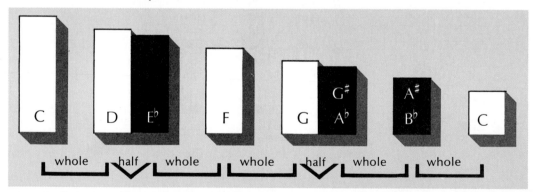

Line up the bells to build a natural minor scale from low C to high C.

Now change the tonality of "Jingle Bells" to minor. Play the melody starting on E♭.

Try building a minor scale from low E to high E. Remember to follow the pattern of whole and half steps shown above.

CALL CHART 10: Chromatic Scale, Whole-Tone Scale

Follow the chart to hear some pieces that make use of the chromatic and whole-tone scales.

1	*CHROMATIC*	Chopin: *Etude,* Op. 10, No. 2
2	*WHOLE-TONE*	Debussy: *Preludes,* "Voiles"
3	*CHROMATIC*	Rimsky-Korsakov: *Flight of the Bumblebee*
4	*CHROMATIC*	Debussy: *Afternoon of a Faun*
5	*CHROMATIC*	Mozart: *String Quartet in D Minor*
6	*WHOLE-TONE*	Rebikov: *Les demons s'amusent*

CALL CHART 11: Major Scale, Minor Scale

Schubert: *Waltz in B minor*

Here is a piece that uses both major and minor scales. The chart will tell you when the melody is based on a major scale and when it is based on a minor scale.

1	*MINOR*
2	*MINOR*
3	*MINOR*
4	*MAJOR*
5	*MINOR*
6	*MAJOR*

159

MAJOR OR MINOR?

One of the spirituals on these pages is based on a major scale.
The other is based on a minor scale. Listen to the recording to
hear which is which.

Rock-a My Soul

BLACK SPIRITUAL   ARRANGED BY JAMES W. ROOKER

For guitar fingerings to play the refrain, see p. 204.

VERSE
SOLO A MIN.   CHORUS
D   A

1. When I went down in the val-ley to pray,   Oh,   rock-a my soul.
2. When I was a mourn-er____ just____ like you, Oh,   rock-a my soul.

SOLO A₇   CHORUS   D.C. al Fine
D

My soul got hap-py and I stayed all day,   Oh,   rock-a my soul.
I mourned and mourned_till____ I come through, Oh,   rock-a my soul.

Joshua Fought the Battle of Jericho

BLACK SPIRITUAL

REFRAIN
D MIN.

1-3. Josh-ua fought the bat-tle of____ Jer-i-cho,____ Jer-i-cho,____

D MIN.

Jer-i-cho,____ Josh-ua fought the bat-tle of____

D MIN.   D MIN. Fine

Jer-i-cho,____ And the walls came tum-bling down!

𝆑 VERSE
D MIN.

1. You may talk a-bout your king of Gid-e-on, You may
2. Then____ up____ to the walls of Jer-i-cho He____
3. Then the lamb,____ ram,____ sheep-horn be-gan to blow, And the

D MIN.   A₇   D MIN.

talk a-bout your man of Saul, There's none like good old
marched____ with a spear in hand, "go blow those ram horns,"
trum-pets be-gan to sound, Then Josh-ua com-mand-ed the

D MIN.   A₇   D MIN. D.C. al Fine

Josh-u-a At the bat-tle of Jer-i-cho.
Josh-ua cried,"'Cause the bat-tle is in my hand."
chil-dren to shout, And the walls____ came tum-bling down.

161

THE PENTATONIC SCALE

Many melodies you sing and play are based, not on a major or minor scale, but on a five-tone scale called *pentatonic*.

To build a G pentatonic scale, start on G and follow this pattern. One of the intervals is a step and a half.

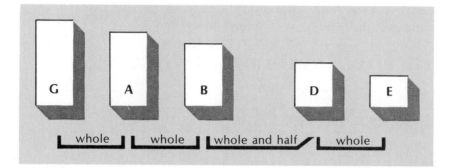

Here is a song based on the G pentatonic scale. To play it, you will need low D and E as well as high D and E.

After lining up the bells you need, try playing the melody as others sing.

Waterbound   TRADITIONAL

Wa - ter - bound,— can't get home,— Wa - ter - bound,— can't get home,

Wa - ter - bound,— can't get home,— Way down in North Ca' - li - na.

2. Chickens a-crowin' from
   an old plough field, (*3 times*)
   Way down in North Ca'lina.

3. Nick and Charlie
   left to go home, (*3 times*)
   Before the water rises.

For guitar fingerings, see p. 204.

Old Texas
OKLAHOMA COWBOY SONG

1. I'm goin' to leave____ old____ Tex - as now,

They've got no use____ for the long - horn cow.____

2. They've plowed and fenced my cattle range,
   And the people there are all so strange.

3. I'll take my horse, I'll take my rope,
   And hit the trail upon a lope.

4. Say *adios* to the Alamo
   And turn my head toward Mexico.

PLAYING ON THE BLACK KEYS

Analyze the intervals of the black keys of the piano.

What scale do they make?

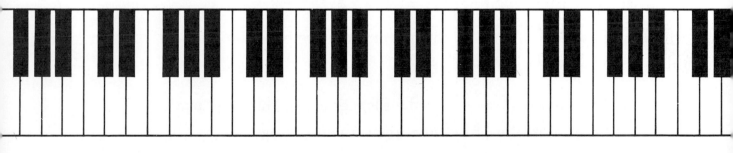

The sets of three and two black keys of the piano have the same arrangement of whole and half steps as the pentatonic scale. Play "Old Texas" by ear, starting on the lower key in the set of two black keys.

 For a recorder ensemble, see p. 207.
 For guitar fingerings, see p. 196.

TONAL—ATONAL

Many composers use all the tones within the octave as a basis for their music. The twelve tones are arranged in a certain order, called a *tone row.*

Each of the twelve tones in a tone row is just as important as all the others. Music based on a tone row is called *atonal.*

Before listening to a piece based on a tone row, arrange the bells so you can play it. Your performance will be part of the piece.

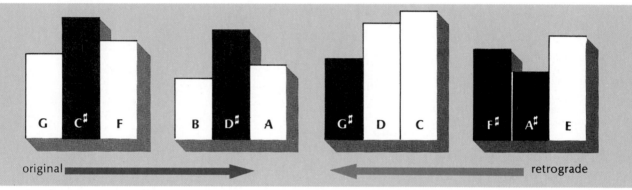

G C♯ F   B D♯ A   G♯ D C   F♯ A♯ E

original ➡   ⬅ retrograde

Group the tones in sets of three, as shown in the picture.

On this recording, you will hear string instruments play each set of three tones as a chord. Fill in the silence after each chord by playing the single tones in the set in any rhythm.

After this section, listen to the rest of the piece based on the same tone row.

At the end (coda), you play in the silences again. This time, play the single tones of each set from right to left (retrograde).

🎵 Eddleman: *Dualisms No. 1*
8

WHAT DO YOU HEAR? 6: Tonality

Listen to the recording. In the first three questions, you will be asked to decide whether the music you hear is tonal or atonal. In questions 4–6, you will be asked to hear whether the tonality stays the same or changes during the piece. In questions 7–9, decide whether the tonality is major or minor.

1	*TONAL*	*ATONAL*
	"I'm Gonna Sing Out"	
2	*TONAL*	*ATONAL*
	Křenek: *Twelve Short Piano Pieces*, "Dancing Toys"	
3	*TONAL*	*ATONAL*
	"He's Got the Whole World in His Hands"	
4	*TONALITY STAYS THE SAME*	*TONALITY CHANGES*
	"Mineira de Minas"	
5	*TONALITY STAYS THE SAME*	*TONALITY CHANGES*
	"It's a Small World"	
6	*TONALITY STAYS THE SAME*	*TONALITY CHANGES*
	"Hallelujah"	
7	*MAJOR*	*MINOR*
	"Rock-a My Soul"	
8	*MAJOR*	*MINOR*
	"Zum Gali Gali"	
9	*MAJOR*	*MINOR*
	"Joshua Fought the Battle of Jericho"	

Style: Music of India

When Western people think of Indian music, they often think of the sitar, a guitar-like instrument made popular by Ravi Shankar.

In India the sitar is used for playing classical music—music improvised on very strict rules of melody (raga) and time measure (tala).

In this example you will hear the sitar accompanied by
a pair of drums, called *tabla*.

After a short section that has no definite rhythm, you will hear
the drum play in a meter of 7. Keep time by clapping the beats
that are marked with an X.

1	2	3	4	5	6	7
X			X		X	

While listening to Indian classical music, the audience keeps time
by clapping and waving their hands. The first beat of the group of 7
is often shown with a wave of the hand or a clap with the back
of the right hand on the palm of the left.

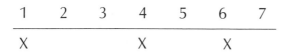 *Raga Yaman*

In addition to Indian classical music, heard mostly in large cities,
the country has a wealth of folk music enjoyed by the villagers.
Small groups of musicians are hired to play "outdoor music"
at weddings, births, and festivals.

Occupational songs are also commonly heard. Farmers sing
as they work in the fields. Woodcutters have their special songs.
Even workmen on a modern building will sometimes chant
as they work.

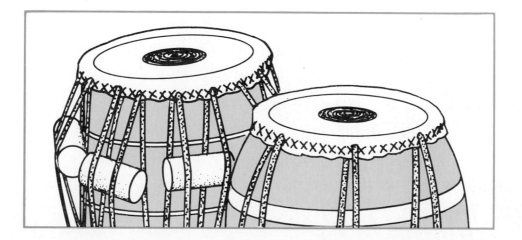

FIVE SONGS FROM INDIA

Here is a folk song from the Sind region, where there is much fishing and trading along the coast. The women sing as they wait for the return of their loved ones, hoping they will bring money and jewels.

As you keep time by clapping, sing the refrain with the recording. *Ho jamalo* means "let us be together again."

🎧 *Ho Jamalo*
6

In this wedding song, the women of the Saora tribe are telling a young bride not to worry that she is leaving home.

🎧 *Saora Wedding Song*
6

How many different tones make up the melody?

Probably the earliest kind of music we know of in India are the religious chants, called the *Veda*. Composed by a tribe of nomadic shepherds, these hymns are sung without any musical instruments for accompaniment.

Listen to the way the singers ornament the melody line as they sing.

🎧 *Sama Vedic Chant*
8

This Hindu religious song tells of King Rama's first meeting with his wife, Sita. It is taken from a very old story of the adventures of King Rama.

Rama was a perfect king—so gentle, kind, and wonderful that the Indians now believe he must have been God disguised as a man.

🎧 *Song from the Ramayana*
8

This religious song is from the Muslim religion. Sing the repeated response "Allah hu," meaning "He is God," when you hear it on the recording.

🎧 *Allah hu*
8

Experiencing the Arts: Perceiving Art

When the arts reach us through our senses, our minds and our feelings get to work.

Our mind pulls together what our senses receive and organizes it. Not only do we see and hear. We notice, we are aware, we discover, we recognize, we remember, we understand. The word for all that is "perceive."

Our feelings are working at the same time. They are excited, aroused, stirred up, moved; we are involved, we are caught up, we respond. The word for all the things our feelings contribute is "react."

FORMULA FOR EXPERIENCING THE ARTS

This formula shows the steps in the process of experiencing art. Use it as you look at the photographs on pages 170 and 171.

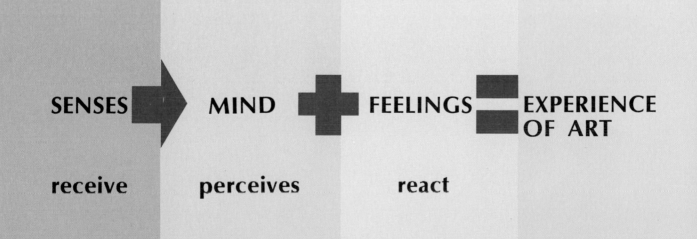

SENSES ➡ MIND ✚ FEELINGS ═ EXPERIENCE OF ART

receive   perceives   react

Van Gogh: THE STARRY NIGHT. Collection, The Museum of Modern Art, New York. Acquired through the Lillie P. Bliss Bequest.

Singing in Chorus

Pavane

LOUIE L. WHITE

*Loo loo loo

loo loo loo loo loo, loo____ loo, loo loo loo loo loo loo loo loo

loo loo loo____

*or some neutral syllable

Loo   loo   loo   loo loo loo loo loo,   loo_____ loo,

loo loo loo loo loo loo loo loo loo_____ loo

Ah_____   ah_____

ah,_____   ah,_____

Fascinating Rhythm

MUSIC BY GEORGE GERSHWIN   WORDS BY IRA GERSHWIN   ARRANGED BY SOL BERKOWITZ

1 Fas - ci - nat - ing rhy - thm, you've got me on the go! Fas - ci -
once it did - n't mat - ter but now you're do - ing wrong; When you

2 Ah _____ Ah _____

1 nat - ing rhy - thm, I'm all a - quiv - er. What a mess you're mak - ing! The
start to pat - ter, I'm so un - hap - py. Won't you take a day off? De -

2 Ah _____ Ah _____ Ah _____

1 neigh - bors want to know why I'm al - ways shak - ing just like a fliv - ver.   Each morn - ing
cide to run a - long some - where far a - way off, and make it snap - py!   Each morn - ing

2 Ah _____ Ah _____   fliv - ver.   Each morn - ing
snap - py!

1 I get up ___ with the sun, Start a - hop - ping, nev - er stop - ping, To find at

2 I get up ___ with the sun, Start a - hop - ping, nev - er stop - ping, To find at

Bless the Beasts and Children

(FROM THE COLUMBIA PICTURES RELEASE: "BLESS THE BEASTS AND CHILDREN")

WORDS AND MUSIC BY BARRY DE VORZON AND PERRY BOTKIN, JR.   ARRANGED BY SOL BERKOWITZ.

Bless the beasts and the chil-dren, for in this world

they have no voice, _____ they have no choice. _____

voice, _____

Bless the beasts and the chil-dren, for the world can nev-er be,

_____ the world they see. _____ Light their way _____

Looks Like Rain in Sunny Lane

WORDS AND MUSIC BY JIMMY CURTISS

1. Oh, you and I _____ lived in hous - es side by side

___ On a street ___ that bore the name ___ of Sun - ny Lane, ___

Sun - ny Lane. ___ We were hap - py there, _____ Had no wor -

- ries, had no cares; ___ Spent each day ___ dream - ing plans, ___

___ and plan - ning dreams, ___ think - ing schemes. ___

REFRAIN

1 Sun - ny Lane, Sun - ny, Sun - ny Lane. ___

MELODY

2 Now it looks like rain in Sun - ny Lane. _____

3 Now it looks like rain in Sun - ny, Sun - ny Lane.

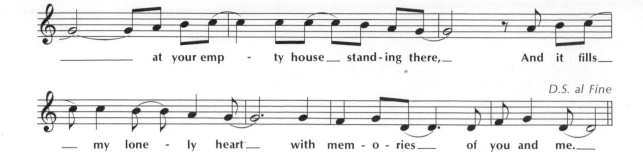

at your emp - ty house___ stand-ing there,___ And it fills___

D.S. al Fine

___ my lone - ly heart___ with mem - o - ries___ of you and me.___

Precious Stones

MUSIC BY JOSEPH GOODMAN   WORDS BY CHRISTINA ROSSETTI

FROM SIX SONGS FOR CHILDREN'S CHORUS BY JOSEPH GOODMAN. COPYRIGHT 1973 GENERAL MUSIC PUBLISHING CO., INC. REPRINTED BY PERMISSION.

An em-'rald is   as green as grass,   A ru - by red as blood, A sap-phire shines as blue as heav'n,___

But a flint

Infinitude

DAVID EDDLEMAN

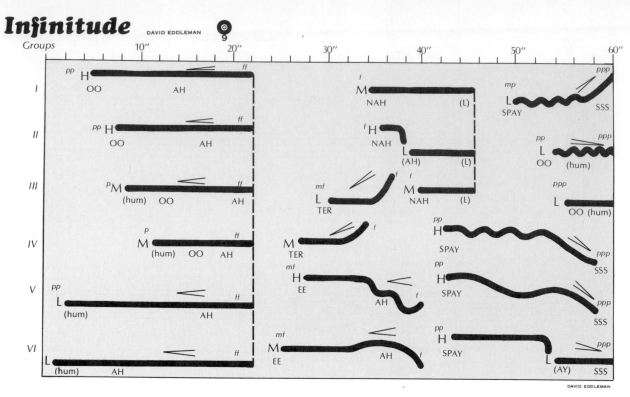

DAVID EDDLEMAN

A conductor will signal at 10-second intervals. Notice that at 22″ (indicated by broken lines), there will be silence for about 2″ ■

At 24″, the words "eternal space" begin in group VI and are fragmented among the other voices ■

Divide the chorus equally into six groups ■ Groups I and II are higher voices, groups III and IV are medium voices, and groups V and VI are lower voices ■

For all groups: H any high note in *your* voice range ■ M any medium note in *your* voice range ■ L any low note in *your* voice range

Each segment is about 10 seconds long ■ Timing is approximate ■

Syllables in capital letters indicate the sound you are to sing ■

Standard symbols are used for dynamic marks ■

After you are assigned to a part, read through it to get an idea of when and how you are to sing ■

DIRECTIONS FOR PERFORMANCE OF "CLEMENTINE"

The electronic music accompaniment for "Clementine" spoofingly changes the pitch up and down at the points marked ∿ ■ Also, the second verse is a half step higher than the first, and the third verse is a half step higher than the second ■ Listen for your new pitch at the start of each new verse ■ At the places marked ∿ try to follow the sounds up and down with your voice, and be sure to return to the right pitch for each verse, just as the accompaniment does ■ The line above the vocal score indicates the accompaniment ■ Although the score calls for the accompaniment and the chorus to begin at the same time, the chorus can also begin at the second measure ■

Clementine

DORIS HAYS

For 2-part chorus with electronic sound accompaniment.   Realized at Queens College Electronic Music Studio.

By Doris Hays © 1973 Tallapoosa Music

TAPE

Clem - en - tine, Clem - en - tine, Clem - en - tine, Clem - en - tine,

1. In a
2. Light she
3. Drove she

cav - ern in a can - yon, Ex - ca - vat - ing for a mine, Dwelt a
was, and like a fair - y, And her shoes were num - ber nine, Her - ring
duck - lings to the wa - ter, Ev - 'ry morn - ing just at nine, Hit her

min - er, for - ty nin - er, And his daugh - ter Clem - en - tine.
box - es with - out top - ses, San - dles were for Clem - en - tine. Oh my
foot a - gainst a splin - ter, Fell in - to the foam - ing brine.

dar - lin', oh my dar - lin', Oh my dar - lin' Clem - en - tine, You are

CODA

lost and gone for - ev - er, dread - ful sor - ry Clem - en - tine.

Simple Gifts

SHAKER HYMN   ARRANGED BY MARILYN DAVIDSON

1 'Tis the gift to be sim - ple, 'Tis the gift to be free, 'Tis the

2 'Tis the gift to be sim - ple, 'Tis the gift to

1 gift to come down where we ought to be, And when we find our-selves__ in the

2 come down where we ought to be, When we find__ our__

1 place just __ right, 'Twill __ be in the val - ley of love and de-light.

2 place just __ right, 'Twill __ be in love and de-light.

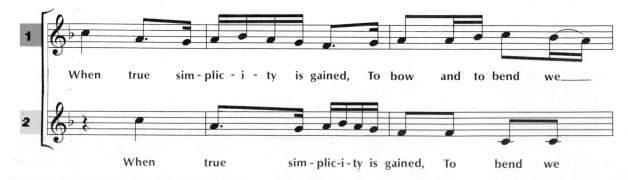

1 When true sim - plic - i - ty is gained, To bow and to bend we__

2 When true sim-plic-i-ty is gained, To bend we

shan't be a-shamed, To turn, turn will be our de-light, Till by

shan't be 'shamed, To___ turn___ will de-light, Till by

turn - ing, turn - ing we come round right.

turn - ing we come round right.

Dona Nobis Pacem (Give Us Peace)

TRADITIONAL ROUND

Do - na no - bis pa - cem, pa - cem, Do - na___

no - bis pa - cem. Do - na no - bis

pa - cem, Do - na no - bis pa - cem. Do - na

no - bis___ pa - cem, Do - na no - bis pa - cem.

All Through the Night

WELSH AIR   VERSE 1 BY HAROLD BOULTON
VERSE 2 ATTRIBUTED TO THOMAS OLIPHANT   ARRANGED BY FRANZ JOSEPH HAYDN

VERSE 1 WORDS REPRINTED BY PERMISSION OF MESSRS. J. B. CRAMER & CO. LTD., LONDON

1. Sleep my child, and peace be with thee All through the night;
2. While the moon her watch is keep-ing All through the night;

Guard-ian an-gels God will send thee All through the night.
While the wea-ry world is sleep-ing All through the night.

Soft the drow-sy hours are creep-ing, Hill and vale in slum-ber steep-ing,
O'er thy spir-it gent-ly steal-ing, Vi-sions of de-light re-veal-ing,

I my lov-ing vig-il keep-ing All through the night.
Breathes a pure and ho-ly feel-ing All through the night.

Playing the Guitar

The guitar has never been more popular nor used more widely than it is today. This satellite will introduce you to guitar playing, beginning with easy chords you can play to accompany singing. Use the recording to hear how your guitar should sound.

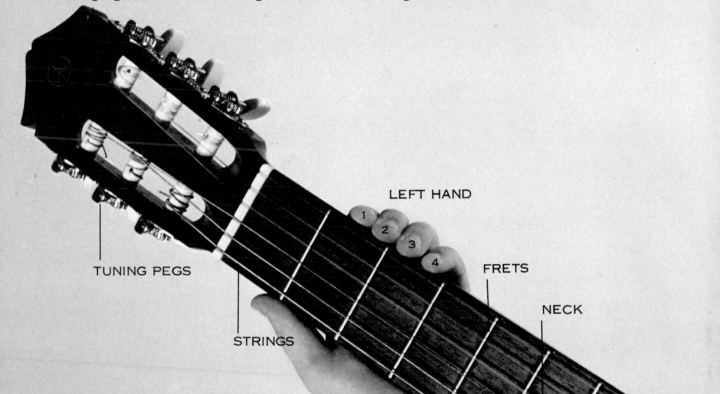

LEFT HAND

TUNING PEGS

FRETS

NECK

STRINGS

This is how the neck of the guitar looks when you are holding it in playing position.

When you first start, it will be easier to have someone tune your guitar for you. Watch carefully to learn how it is done, then try tuning it by yourself and have someone check what you have done.

THE E-MINOR CHORD

A drawing of the top of the guitar's neck is used to show where to put your fingers on the strings. Compare the drawing with the photograph.

In this satellite, only the strings shown in red on the diagram are to be strummed. In the E Minor chord, all six strings are strummed.

When you are ready, play these three songs. Strum with the thumb of your right hand each time a small stroke (/) appears over the music.

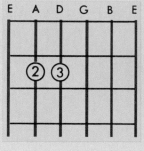

Shalom, Chaverim
ISRAELI ROUND

E MIN.

Sha - lom, cha - ver - im! Sha - lom cha - ver - im! sha - lom, sha - lom. Le -

hit - ra - ot, le - hit - ra - ot, sha - lom,_____ sha - lom.

Hey, Ho! Nobody Home
OLD ENGLISH ROUND

E MIN.

Hey, ho! No - bo - dy home. Meat nor drink nor mon - ey have I none,

Yet I will be mer - ry.__ Hey, ho! No - bo - dy home.

Jane, Jane

AMERICAN FOLK SONG   REPRINTED FROM SING OUT!—THE FOLK SONG MAGAZINE. USED WITH PERMISSION.

Make up your own pattern of strumming for this song. Rap
lightly on the body of the guitar instead of playing chords each
time you sing the words *Jane, Jane.*

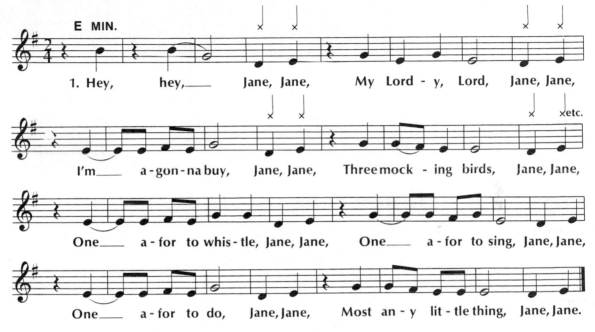

E MIN.

1. Hey,   hey,____   Jane, Jane,   My Lord - y, Lord,   Jane, Jane,

I'm____   a - gon - na buy,   Jane, Jane,   Three mock - ing birds,   Jane, Jane,

One____   a - for to whis - tle, Jane, Jane,   One____ a - for to sing, Jane, Jane,

One____   a - for to do,   Jane, Jane,   Most an - y lit - tle thing, Jane, Jane.

2. Hey, hey, Jane, Jane,
   My Lordy, Lord, Jane, Jane,
   I'm a-gonna buy, Jane, Jane,
   Three hunting dogs, Jane, Jane,
   One a-for to run, Jane, Jane,
   One a-for to shout, Jane, Jane,
   One to talk to, Jane, Jane,
   When I go out, Jane, Jane.

3. Hey, hey, . . .
   My Lordy, Lord, . . .
   I'm a-gonna buy, . . .
   Three muley cows, . . .
   One a-for to milk, . . .
   One to plough my corn, . . .
   One a-for to pray, . . .
   One Christmas morn, . . .

4. Hey, hey, . . .
   My Lordy, Lord, . . .
   I'm a-gonna buy, . . .
   Three little blue birds, . . .
   One a-for to weep, . . .
   One a-for to mourn, . . .
   One a-for to grieve, . . .
   When I am gone, . . .

THE C CHORD

To play the C chord, put
finger 1, your index
finger, on the B string,
first fret. Strum the
strings shown in red.

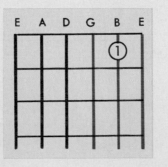

THE G₇ CHORD

To play the G₇ chord, place finger 1 on the high E string, first fret, and strum the strings shown in red.

When you can play the G₇ chord, practice changing from C to G₇ and back until you can do it easily. Then you are ready to play this song. Notice that the chord changes each time you sing the word *money*.

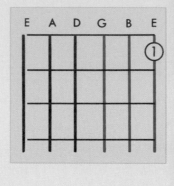

Pay Me My Money Down

SLAVE SONG FROM THE GEORGIA SEA ISLANDS COLLECTED AND ADAPTED BY LYDIA A. PARRISH

1. I thought I heard the cap-tain say, "Pay me my mon-ey down,___
To-mor-row is our sail-ing day,___ Pay me my mon-ey down."_
"Pay___ me,___ oh, pay___ me, ___ Pay me my mon-ey down,_
Pay me or go to jail,___ Pay me my mon-ey down."_

2. As soon as the boat was clear of the bar,
   "Pay me my money down,"
   He knocked me down with the end of a spar,
   "Pay me my money down." *Refrain*

3. Well, I wish I was Mr. Steven's son,
   "Pay me my money down,"
   Sit on the bank and watch the work done,
   "Pay me my money down." *Refrain*

INTRODUCING THE BASS GUITAR

When you can play the song to accompany singing, or to accompany the recording, team up with a friend to play these parts for two guitars. The player who strums the chords is called the "lead" guitar. Another player, who plays only single tones on the low-sounding strings, is called the "bass."

BASS GUITAR: Finger the E and A strings as shown. These will not be chords! The bass guitar player plays single tones only.

When the chord is C, alternate the A and E strings in each measure. You are playing the tones C and G.

When the chord is G_7, alternate the E and D strings in each measure. You are playing the tones G and D.

Here is a guitar part you can play to accompany the singing of a familiar song. Lead guitar plays chords in the rhythm shown or one the player chooses. Bass guitar plays single tones.

He's Got the Whole World in His Hands BLACK SPIRITUAL

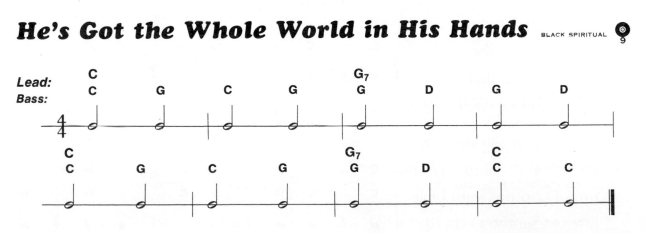

Streets of Laredo

AMERICAN COWBOY SONG

Team up with a friend. One of you plays the lead guitar part while the other plays the bass guitar part.

LEAD GUITAR: Try varying the rhythm. Strum down with the thumb and up with the fingers.

BASS GUITAR: For variety, play the tone for each chord on the first and third beats of each measure.

When changing from the G_7 to the C chord, play the tone D on the third beat just before the C chord.

Buffalo Gals

AMERICAN FOLK SONG

Here is another song using the C and G₇ chords.

1. As I was walk-ing down the street, down the street, down the street, A
2. I asked her if she'd stop and talk, stop and talk, stop and talk, Her

pret-ty lit-tle girl I chanced to meet, un-der the sil-very moon._____
feet___ took___ up the whole side-walk, she was___ fair to view._____

Buf-fa-lo gals won't you come out to-night, come out to-night, come out to-night?

Buf-fa-lo gals won't you come out to-night and dance by the light of the moon?___

Skip to My Lou

AMERICAN GAME SONG

1. Flies in the butter-milk, shoo, fly, shoo! Flies in the butter-milk, shoo, fly, shoo!
2. Little red wag-on paint-ed blue, Little red wag-on paint-ed blue,

Flies in the butter-milk, shoo, fly, shoo!
Little red wag-on paint-ed blue, Skip to my Lou, my dar-ling.

3. Lost my partner, what'll I do? . . .

4. I'll get another, better than you! . . .

THE G CHORD

Look at the diagram to figure out how to play a simple G chord. The photograph will help you.

Strum the strings shown in red. You can also include the D string in the chord for a fuller sound.

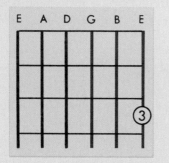

THE D₇ CHORD

Here is the diagram showing how to finger the D_7 chord. Strum the strings shown in red. You can also include the A string in the chord for a fuller sound.

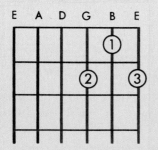

Try changing back and forth between D_7 and G. When you can make the change as smoothly as possible, try the following songs with the recording.

Down in the Valley

KENTUCKY FOLK SONG

1. Down in the val - ley, The val - ley so low,_____
2. Writ - ing a let - ter con - tain - ing three lines,_____

Hang your head o - ver, hear the wind blow._____
An - swer my ques - tion, "Will you be mine?_____

Hear the wind blow, dear, hear the wind blow,_____
Will you be mine, dear, Will you be mine,_____

Hang your head o - ver, hear the wind blow._____
An - swer my ques - tion, Will you be mine?"_____

Clementine

AMERICAN FOLK SONG

Oh, my dar - lin', oh, my dar - lin', Oh my dar - lin' Clem - en - tine,

You are lost and gone for-ev - er, Dread - ful sor - ry, Clem-en - tine.

BASS GUITAR: Try to always play the root of the chord (G for the G chord; D for the D_7 chord) on the first beat when the chord changes.

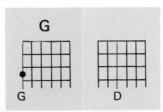

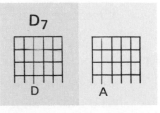

Oh, Won't You Sit Down?

BLACK SPIRITUAL

Here is another song to help you to practice the G and D₇ chords. When the bass and lead guitars can accompany the singing, add handclaps, tambourine, or other percussion to the performance.

REFRAIN

G

Oh, won't you sit down?__ Lord, I can't sit down.__ Oh, won't you

G   D₇

sit down?__ Lord, I can't sit down.__ Oh, won't you

G   D₇

sit down?__ Lord, I can't sit down.__ 'Cause I

G   D₇   G   Fine

just got to Heav-en, gon-na look a-round.__

VERSE

1. Who's that yon-der dressed in red?____

G   D₇   G

Must be the chil-dren that____ Mo-ses led.__

G

Who's that yon-der dressed in white?____ *D.C. al Fine*

G   D₇   G

Must be the chil-dren of the Is-rael-ite.__

2. Who's that yonder dressed in blue?

Must be the children that are comin' through.

Who's that yonder dressed in black?

Must be the hypocrites a-turnin' back. *Refrain*

PLAYING WITH THREE CHORDS

Many songs need at least three chords. With G, C, and D_7 (the G family) you can play a wide selection of songs.

Practice changing from one chord in the G family to another so you can accompany the next three songs. Strum on each beat or make up a rhythm pattern of your own.

BASS GUITAR: Alternate the bass strings shown for each chord. Play on the strong beat of each measure. Remember, play the root (the note with the same name as the chord) on the first beat when the chord changes.

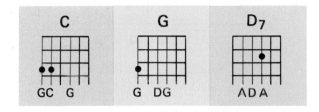

She'll Be Comin' Round the Mountain

SOUTHERN MOUNTAIN SONG

1. She'll be com - in' round the moun - tain when she comes, She'll be

com - in' round the moun - tain when she comes, She'll be

com - in' round the moun-tain, She'll be com - in' round the moun-tain, She'll be

com - in' round the moun-tain when she comes.

2. She'll be drivin' six white horses when she comes, . . .
3. Oh, we'll kill the old red rooster when she comes, . . .
4. Oh, we'll all have chicken and dumplings when she comes, . . .
5. Oh, we'll all go out to meet her when she comes, . . .

PLAYING WITH FOUR CHORDS

"Mama Don't 'Low" uses the chords G, D_7, G_7, and C. Listen to the recording to see how the chords fit the music. After you have learned "Mama Don't 'Low," you can add a bass guitar part played by a friend.

BASS GUITAR: Alternate the bass strings shown for each chord.

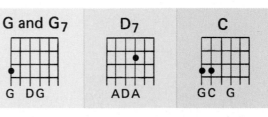

LEAD GUITAR: Vary the rhythm of your strumming. Choose one of these rhythms.

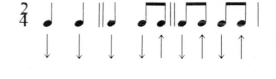

Mama Don't 'Low

AMERICAN FOLK SONG

1.
2. } Ma - ma don't 'low no { gui - tar play - in' round here,_____
3.   rock song sing - in' round here,_____
      ban - jo pick - in' round here,_____

Ma - ma don't 'low no { gui - tar play - in' round here,_____
                         ban - jo pick - in' round here,_____
                         rock song sing - in' round here,_____

I don't care what Ma - ma don't 'low, Gon-na { play my gui - tar an - y - how,
                                                pick my ban - jo an - y - how,
                                                sing my rock songs an - y - how,

Ma - ma don't 'low no { gui - tar play - in' round here._____
                         ban - jo pick - in' round here._____
                         rock song sing - in' round here._____

THE D CHORD

Listen to the sound of the D chord on the recording, then try it yourself.

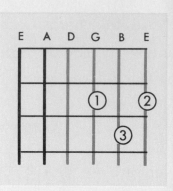

THE A₇ CHORD

The A₇ chord uses all six strings. To change from the D chord to the A₇ chord, lift fingers 1 and 2 of your left hand and move them one string toward you, staying in the second fret.

BASS GUITAR: Alternate the bass strings shown for each chord.

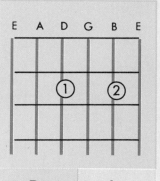

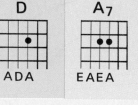

Tom Dooley AMERICAN FOLK SONG

1. Hang down your head, Tom Dool - ey, Hang down your head and cry,
2. This_____ time to - mor - row, Wond-er ____ where I'll be?

Hang down your head, Tom Dool - ey, Poor boy, you're bound to die.
Down in some lone - some val - ley Hang-in' from a white oak tree.

When the Saints Go Marching In

BLACK SPIRITUAL 9

Here is a four-chord song using D and A_7.

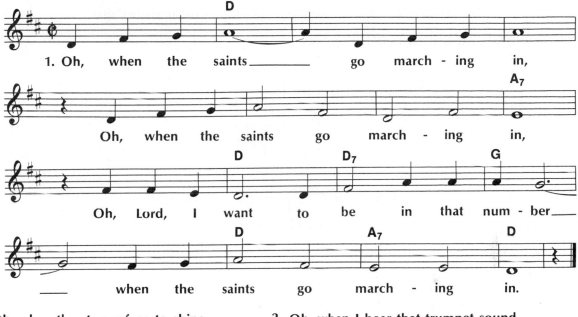

1. Oh, when the saints _____ go march - ing in,
Oh, when the saints go march - ing in,
Oh, Lord, I want to be in that num - ber____
_____ when the saints go march - ing in.

2. Oh, when the stars refuse to shine, . . .   **3.** Oh, when I hear that trumpet sound, . . .

HAVE A SING-A-LONG

Using the chords you have learned in this satellite, you can play these songs in *Silver Burdett Music 5.*

E MINOR
Toembaï, p. 10
Zum Gali Gali, p. 136

C, G_7
Nani Wale Na Hala, p. 118
Everybody Loves Saturday Night, p. 134

G, D_7
Banana Boat Loaders, p. 55
Old Texas, p. 163

D, A_7
Water Come a Me Eye, p. 84
Rock-a My Soul (Refrain), p. 160

D, G, A_7
Vive la Canadienne!, p. 11
Streets of Laredo, p. 71
Winds of Morning, p. 92
Island Hopping, p. 148

G, D_7, A_7
Mineira de Minas, p. 20

G, D_7, C
It's a Small World, p. 48
The Lord Is My Shepherd, p. 155
Waterbound, p. 162

D, A_7, D_7, G
The Hammer Song, p. 86

CHORD CHART

Here are all the chords you have learned in this satellite. The strings to be strummed are shown in red. Bass guitar notes are shown at the bottom of this page.

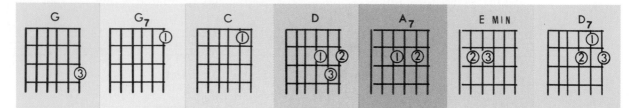

The fingerings you learned for G, G₇, and C are simplified fingerings. Here are the complete chords.

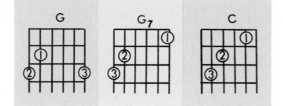

BASS GUITAR

The four strings of a bass guitar are tuned to the same pitches as the four lowest-sounding strings of a six-string guitar. These diagrams show all the <u>single tones</u> that you can choose to play for each chord shown.

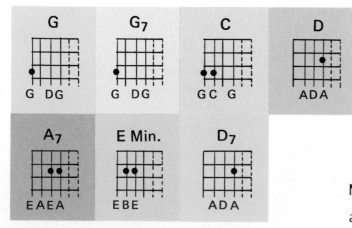

Note: These diagrams show some additional possibilities.

Playing the Recorder 🎯

COVER-THE-HOLE TEST

Hold the recorder with both hands, as pictured. Make sure your left hand is above your right. Press just hard enough so that the hole will make a light mark on each finger and on the thumb of your left hand.

MAKING A SOUND

Cover the tip of the mouthpiece with your lips. Your teeth should not touch the recorder. Blow gently through the recorder, starting to blow with a "daah."

Alto Recorder

Soprano Recorder

PRIVATE PRACTICE

Now you are ready to work with the fingerings. A diagram of the holes is used to show where to place your fingers to play the pitch. Each hole is covered by one specific finger and no other.

Experiment with each new pitch until your fingers feel secure. Play rhythm patterns of songs you know or improvise (make up) your own.

THREE NOTES TO BEGIN

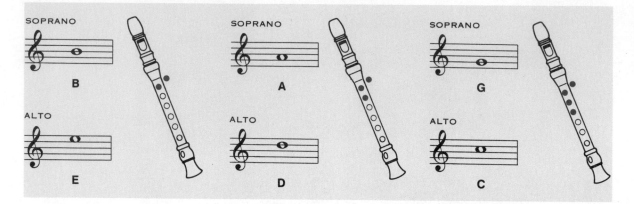

PRIVATE PRACTICE

Play the notes B, A, and G on the soprano recorder,

E, D, and C on the alto recorder.

Then try these three-note melodies. First, listen to the recording.
Follow the score and finger the notes without playing. Then
play the melody by yourself or with the recording.

Hot Cross Buns TRADITIONAL

Chong Chong Nai MALAYSIAN FOLK TUNE © 1974 OXFORD UNIVERSITY PRESS

FIRST ENSEMBLES

Ensemble playing means playing in a group, carefully fitting different parts together to make musical sense. When playing in ensembles, you must listen to the other parts as you play.

Mama Don't 'Low (SONG ON PAGE 4)

Old Texas (SONG ON PAGE 163)

For a larger ensemble, ask someone to play an Autoharp or guitar accompaniment. Ask others to sing.

TWO NEW NOTES

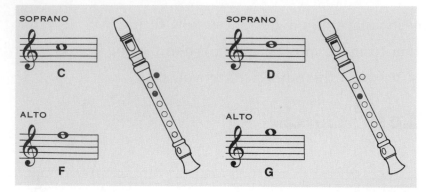

PRIVATE PRACTICE

Now you can play five notes. Practice them and try the next
two melodies. Play your part while others sing the song and
play chords on an Autoharp.

Jingle Bells   JAMES PIERPONT

Lady, Come  FOLK SONG FROM ENGLAND

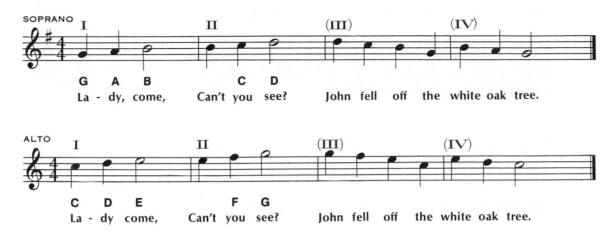

When you play the melody alone, try it as a round. Choose others to play with you.

MORE ENSEMBLES

On Top of Old Smoky (SONG ON P. 64)

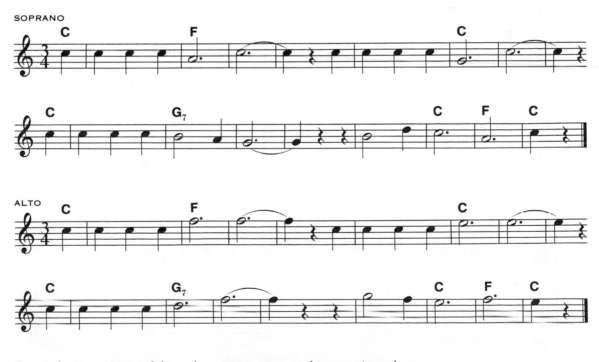

For a larger ensemble ask someone to play an Autoharp or guitar accompaniment. Ask others to sing.

Pay Me My Money Down (SONG ON P. 70)

Practice this part to play while others sing.

When the Saints Go Marching In

Practice the melody on a soprano recorder. Ask someone to play the countermelody on the alto recorder.

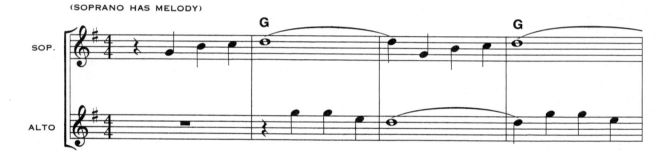

For a larger ensemble ask someone to play an Autoharp or guitar accompaniment. Ask others to sing.

Pay Me My Money Down (SONG ON P. 70)

Practice this part to play while others sing.

For a larger ensemble ask someone to play the soprano part on
p. 210. Add an Autoharp or guitar accompaniment.

When the Saints Go Marching In

Practice the melody on an alto recorder. Ask someone to play
the countermelody on a soprano recorder.

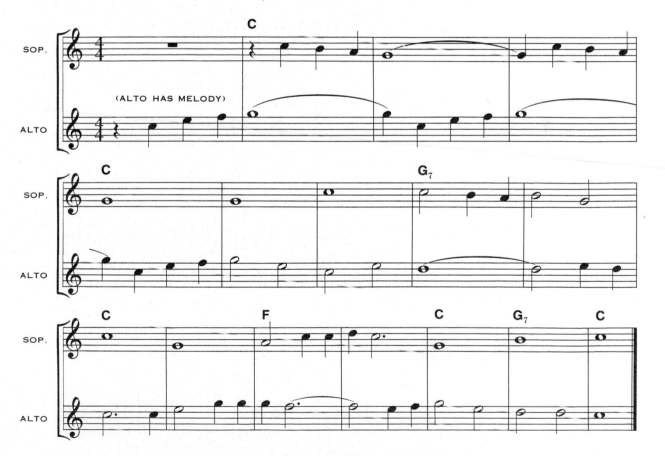

For a larger ensemble ask someone to play an Autoharp
accompaniment. Ask others to sing.

TWO MORE NEW NOTES

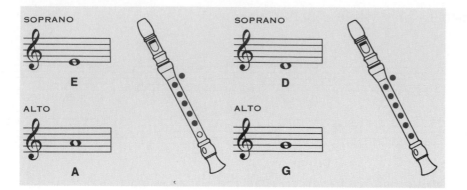

SOPRANO — E
ALTO — A

SOPRANO — D
ALTO — G

PRIVATE PRACTICE

Fishpole Song SOUTHERN SINGING GAME

This melody uses notes you know on the soprano recorder.

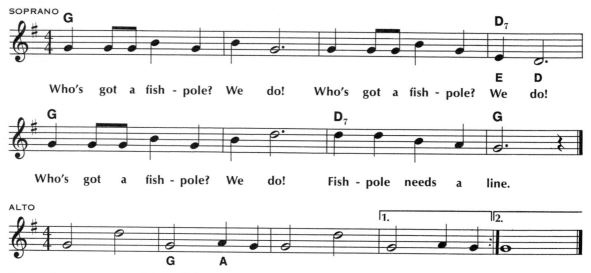

Who's got a fish - pole? We do! Who's got a fish - pole? We do!

Who's got a fish - pole? We do! Fish - pole needs a line.

For a larger ensemble add Autoharp or guitar accompaniment while others sing.

TRY THIS

While others sing, play this part on soprano and alto recorders each time it comes in the song "Jane, Jane." (The song is found in the Playing the Guitar satellite, page 191.)

SOPRANO

ALTO

Jane, Jane

Jane, Jane

Fishpole Song

This melody uses notes you know on the alto recorder.

Who's got a fish - pole? We do! Who's got a fish - pole? We do!

Who's got a fish - pole? We do! Fish - pole needs a line.

Choose someone to play the soprano recorder with you.

For a larger ensemble add Autoharp or guitar accompaniment while others sing.

Morning Bells FOLK MELODY FROM GERMANY

This round uses notes you know on the soprano recorder. Play it alone and as a round with others.

MORE ENSEMBLES

Add the tone color of an alto recorder to the ensemble.

Add the tone color of a triangle to the ensemble. Play on the first beat of every measure.

Oh, Won't You Sit Down?

Try playing the melody on p. 198 in the Playing the Guitar satellite. It uses these notes on the soprano recorder.

D E G A B

ENSEMBLE

Here are two countermelodies that can be played with the melody, one for soprano recorder, the other for alto recorder.

Put as many parts together as you can: voices, recorders, guitar, Autoharp. Add hand claps, tambourine, and other percussion instruments to the performance.

ANOTHER NEW NOTE

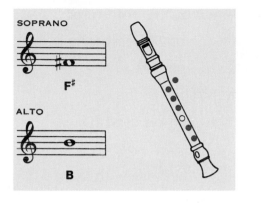

This repeated pattern, called an **ostinato,** uses a new note, F♯. Practice it on the soprano recorder.

G   F♯   E   D

Use the ostinato when another soprano recorder plays "Fishpole Song" on p. 212 and "Oh, Won't You Sit Down," Playing the Guitar satellite, p. 198.

Practice this ostinato on an alto recorder. It uses a new note, B.

ALTO

C   B   A   G

Ask someone who plays the alto recorder to play "Fishpole Song" on p. 213 while you play the ostinato.

ENSEMBLE

After you can play this melody, team up with two, three, or four friends who play the soprano recorder. Play the melody through at least two times. Then play it as a round. Parts II, III, and IV follow in turn two measures apart.

Tallis' Canon THOMAS TALLIS

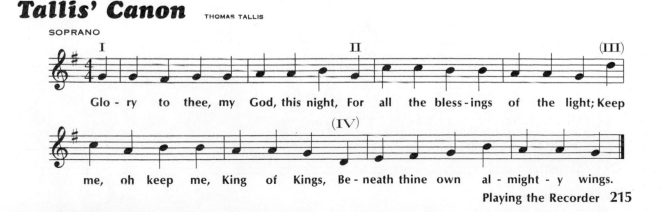

SOPRANO

I   II   (III)

Glo-ry   to   thee,   my   God, this night, For   all   the   bless-ings   of   the   light; Keep

(IV)

me,   oh   keep   me,   King   of   Kings,   Be-neath thine   own   al-might-y   wings.

RECORDER SOUND PIECE 1: Notes and Rhythms

1. Copy the staff (5 lines and 4 spaces) as shown at the bottom of the page. Be sure to include the bar lines, which show measures.

2. Lightly draw a pitch for each measure. Use the pitches in the first column if you play soprano recorder, the pitches in the second column if you play alto recorder. Pitches can be used more than once.

3. Using the pitch you have selected, fill in each measure with a rhythm pattern from the third column. Each pattern may be used more than once.

4. Play your melody.

5. For an ensemble, team up with someone who has made up a melody on either a soprano or alto recorder. Play the melodies alone, one after the other (A B form). Then change the texture by playing both melodies together.

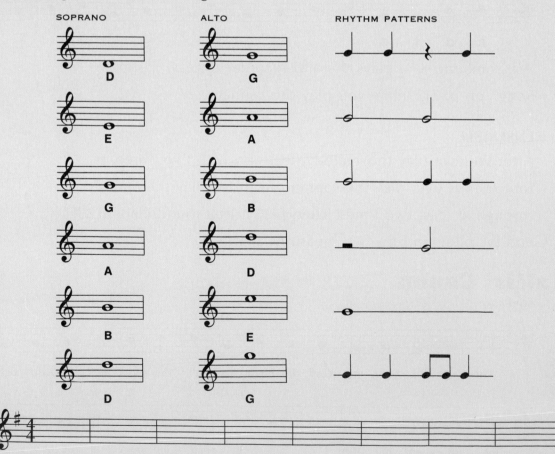

PRIVATE PRACTICE FOR SOPRANO RECORDER

Now that you know the fingering for F#, you can play the melodies of the following songs on the soprano recorder.

- Clementine, p. 197
- Down in the Valley, p. 197
- It's a Small World (Section B), p. 48
- Water Come a Me Eye, p. 84
- When the Saints Go Marching In, p. 203

PRIVATE PRACTICE FOR ALTO RECORDER

For more practice using the new note, B, alto recorder players can play the melody of the following songs, reading from the soprano recorder scores.

- Hot Cross Buns, p. 206
- Chong Chong Nai, p. 206
- Jingle Bells, p. 208
- Lady Come, p. 209
- When the Saints Go Marching In, p. 210

ENSEMBLES FOR ALTO RECORDERS

For an ensemble using only alto recorders, combine any of the parts on the following pages.

- Mama Don't 'Low, p. 207
- Old Texas, p. 207
- On Top of Old Smoky, p. 209
- Pay Me My Money Down, pp. 210, 211
- When the Saints Go Marching In, pp. 210, 211

Add Autoharp, guitar, or percussion instruments to the ensemble.

ANOTHER NEW NOTE

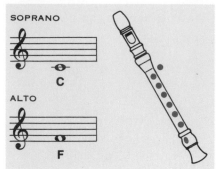

SOPRANO
C

ALTO
F

PRIVATE PRACTICE

Before playing this song, find the new note in the score for the
recorder you play.

Hop Up and Jump Up SHAKER MELODY

ENSEMBLE

For an ensemble, play your parts as others sing and dance. (See
Responding Through Movement, p. 246.)

La Cucaracha

RECORDER SOUND PIECE 2: Creating a Melody

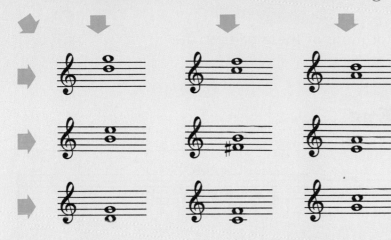

You know how to play nine tones on the recorder. Use these tones to make up your own melody.

Follow the arrows to play a sequence of notes in any order.

The upper note on each staff is for alto recorder; the lower note for soprano.

When you have worked out a sequence of notes, add your own rhythm pattern for each box. Another time, change the meter. Play rhythm patterns in 3 meter, then in 2 meter.

PRIVATE PRACTICE

The Bird's Song ROUND FROM QUEBEC

ENSEMBLE

• Play melody as a two-part round on soprano recorder, alto recorder, or both. Then try playing it as a round in three or four parts.

• Add the Autoharp or guitar to the ensemble.

• Play melody while others add ostinatos below on recorders or bells.

FINAL ENSEMBLE

While others sing, add one or more of these parts to the ensemble.

Water Come a Me Eye (SONG ON P. 84)

Reading Rhythm

Have you ever heard a train's wheels as they "clack-clack-clacked" along the track? Or a wrist watch tick-tocking away? Or a leaky faucet going "drip-drip-drip?" You probably noticed the way the sounds repeated at exactly the same length of time.

BEAT

What you heard and felt was a basic element of rhythm: *beat*. In music, the beat, also called the *pulse,* can be represented by a single note. Listen to the following beat pattern. Follow each beat, here represented by a *quarter note*

In much of the music you sing there is a beat that goes on and on. If the music gets faster or slows down, it is because the beat gets faster or slows down.

STEADY BEAT; QUARTER NOTES

You can play each beat in the song "Mama Don't 'Low," page 4, while others sing or while you follow the recording. Play the beats on a woodblock while following this score. Notice that the beats are grouped in sets of two. The vertical lines are called *bars,* or *barlines,* and the distance between barlines is called a *measure.*

Mama Don't 'Low (SEE PAGE 4.)

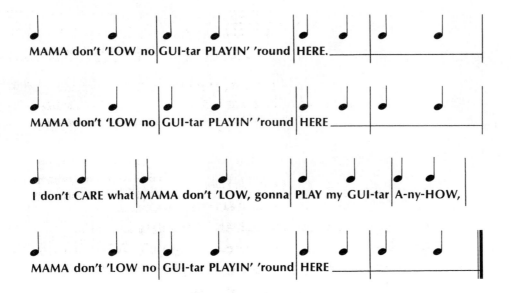

Experiment with other ways to play beats to accompany "Mama Don't 'Low." For example, tap your toe on one beat and clap on the next beat.

HALF NOTES

Team up with a friend. While you play every beat on a woodblock (two in each measure), your friend plays on a triangle a note that lasts for two beats—the entire measure.

The note that is being held through two beats is called a *half note* (♩). The length (duration) of this note is equal to two quarter notes when they are tied together (♩ = ♪♪). Here is a part for two players, to accompany "I'm Gonna Sing Out," page 24. One plays high and low temple blocks, or two woodblocks, the other a triangle. What notes are used in the score?

I'm Gonna Sing Out

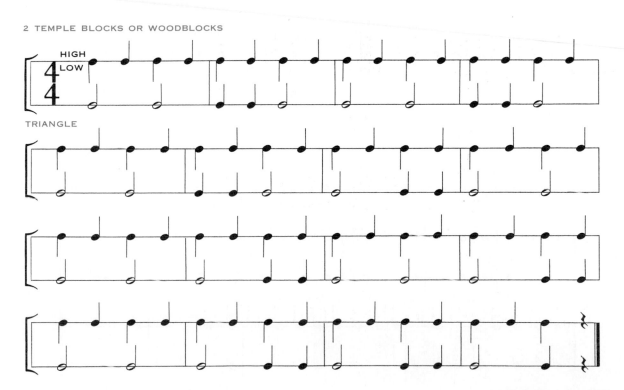

METER SIGNATURE

The *meter signature*—the numbers that appear at the beginning of a musical composition—tells you two things about the rhythm of the music. The top number tells *how many* beats are in each measure; the bottom number tells what note represents *one* beat.

> 2 = 2 BEATS IN EACH MEASURE
>
> 4 = A QUARTER NOTE REPRESENTS ONE BEAT
>
> 3 = 3 BEATS IN EACH MEASURE
>
> 4 = A QUARTER NOTE REPRESENTS ONE BEAT
>
> 4 = 4 BEATS IN EACH MEASURE
>
> 4 = A QUARTER NOTE REPRESENTS ONE BEAT

Practice this part for gourd (or bongo) and guiro. Two players can accompany "Mineira de Minas," page 20, while others sing or as you listen to the recording. If stereo is available, use Pick-a-Track to hear how both rhythm patterns sound when played together. Be careful; this song begins in $\frac{3}{4}$ and changes to $\frac{4}{4}$.

Mineira de Minas (SEE PAGE 20.)

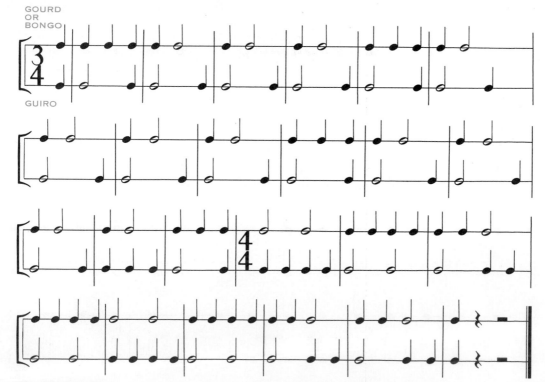

EIGHTH NOTES

You may already know that two eighth notes (♫ or ♪♪) are equal to one quarter note (♫ = ♩). Listen to the following rhythm pattern on the recording to hear how eighths and quarters fit together.

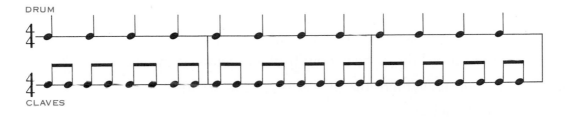

Now play the following part on claves. It uses both quarter and eighth notes. After practicing the part, add it to the ensemble on page 224 while others sing, or as you follow the recording. Watch for the change to $\frac{4}{4}$ in the middle of the song.

THIRD PART TO

Mineira de Minas

TRIPLETS

In "Mineira de Minas" you played two eighth notes on one beat. Sometimes three equal notes are played in the space of one beat. These are called *triplets*. Triplets usually have a small 3 over the notes:♫. Speak the word "merrily" several times while clapping a steady beat on the first syllable. You will be speaking triplets.

Listen to the recording to hear how triplets divide each beat into three sounds. Which instrument plays the steady beat? Which plays triplets?

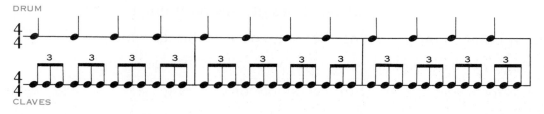

"Look Out!" by Doris Hays, is another song in which the meter changes, but this time it changes in every measure, following this pattern: |2 beats |3 beats |4 beats|.

Practice this arrangement for triangle, finger cymbals, and temple blocks or woodblock, to play with the song "Look Out!"

Look Out   DORIS HAYS

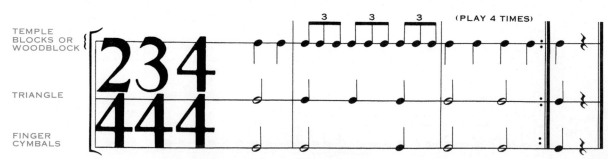

This part for "Pat-a-Pan," page 27, may be played on a drum using your hands. Notice that each half note is notated ♪. The three slashes through the stem indicate a *roll* (very fast hits) on the drum head for the duration of the half note.

Pat-a-Pan

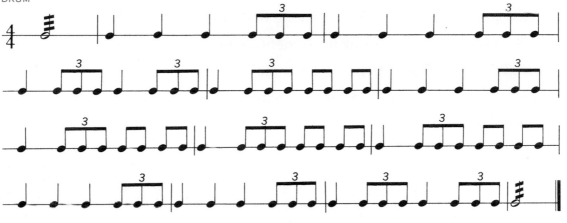

RESTS

Rhythm patterns are made of sounds and silences. Just as there are symbols for each duration of sound, there are symbols for each duration of silence, or rest.

The following part uses both sounds and rests. Practice this part to accompany the singing of "Zigy, Zigy, Za," page 58.

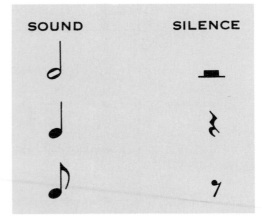

SOUND	SILENCE

Zigy, Zigy, Za   (THE SYMBOL > TELLS YOU TO STRESS OR <u>ACCENT</u> THAT NOTE.)

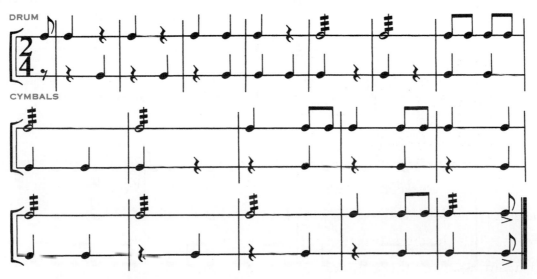

Tzena, Tzena

Try using what you know by playing rhythms on instruments. This ensemble, or group of instruments, can accompany the song "Tzena, Tzena," page 50. Each player in the ensemble selects one part to play. After practicing your part at home or in school, add it to another until all parts are playing. If you need help, listen to the recording.

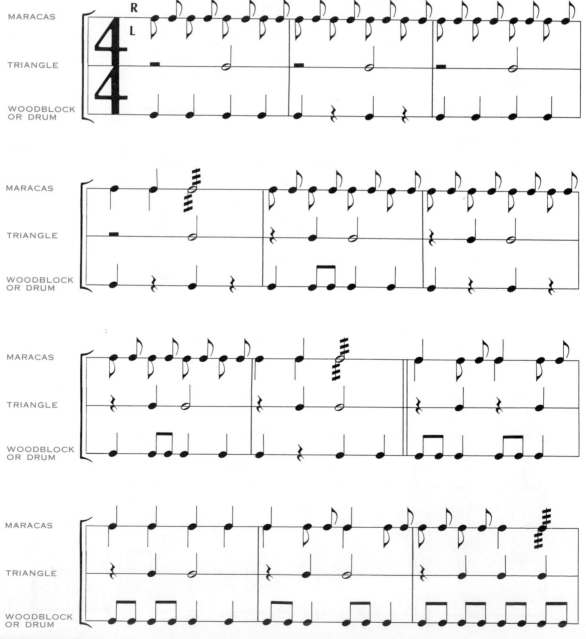

SIXTEENTH NOTES

If you can divide by two, you can understand the system used in notating rhythm patterns. Just as the half note (♩) can be divided into two quarter notes (♩ = ♩♩), and a quarter note into two eighth notes (♩ = ♫), so an eighth note can be divided into two sixteenths (♪ = ♪♪ or ♬). Listen to the recording to hear how sixteenths sound against half, quarter, and eighth notes.

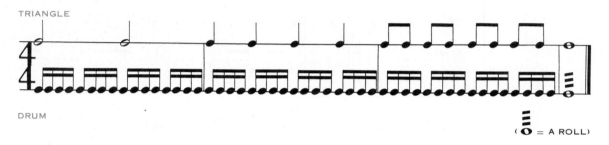

The longest sound in the last measure is a *whole note* (o). Its sound lasts the whole measure. In the meter $\frac{4}{4}$, how many beats will this note last?

Look at this drum part for "Deep Blue Sea," page 66. What notations do you find? You should see $\frac{4}{4}$, $\frac{2}{4}$, ♩, ♪, ♬, , | |, and >. If you know how to perform all these symbols in sound, practice the part to accompany the song. Be sure the sixteenth notes are played evenly—four sounds to one beat.

Deep Blue Sea (SEE PAGE 66.)

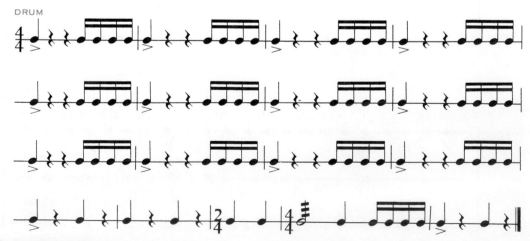

Thank God, I'm a Country Boy

Here is an ensemble you and your friends can play to accompany "Thank God, I'm a Country Boy," page 68. Listen to the recording, then try it yourself. If stereo is available, use Pick-a-Track to hear how both rhythm patterns sound when played together.

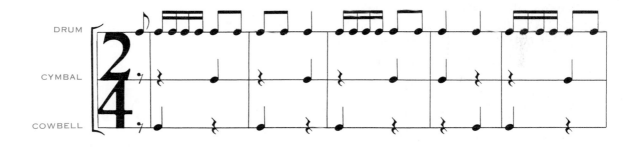

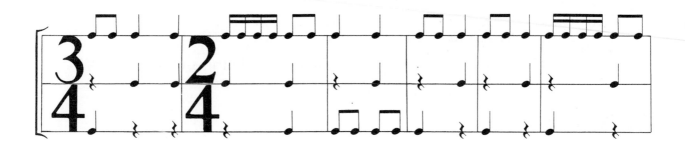

DOTTED RHYTHMS

A dot after a note makes it longer by half its value. Look at the following table for an easy way to think of dotted rhythms.

Do you notice that the dot takes place of the tie? What would a dotted half (♩.) equal? What would a dotted quarter (♩.) equal? Listen to these patterns on the recording. First, you will hear the steady beat, then you will hear each pattern played three times.

The rhythm pattern in this ensemble to accompany "The Hammer Song," page 86, uses two of the dotted rhythms above, as well as quarter notes and quarter rests.

The Hammer Song (SEE PAGE 86.)

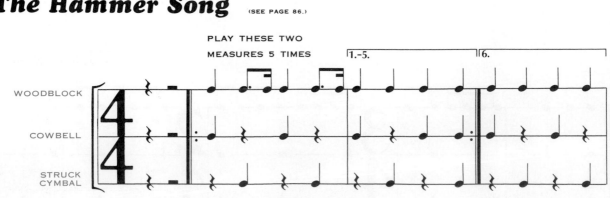

Try playing another accompaniment that uses dotted rhythms to play with "The Ocean Waves," page 129. Form an ensemble of instruments and singers to perform this piece.

The Ocean Waves

SYNCOPATION

Listen to the following pattern on the recording.

The pattern in the first half of each measure is called *syncopation.* The special feeling of syncopation comes from playing a note on the weak part of the beat and holding it through the strong beat. The syncopated notes fall *between* the steady beats.

The following part played on a tambourine can accompany "Vine and Fig Tree," page 137. Find the measures that use syncopation. Listen to the recording to hear how the syncopation fits the steady beat, then try playing the part yourself.

Vine and Fig Tree

TAMBOURINE

The next score also contains syncopation as well as other rhythm patterns you have studied in this satellite.

Matilda

REVIEW ENSEMBLE

Choose one of the parts in the arrangement below and practice
it with the recording. Then organize a group of your classmates
and play the entire "Review Ensemble."

Responding Through Movement

When you move to music you respond to some of the same qualities as when you sing and play.

- TEMPO
- METER
- STEADY BEAT
- PHRASING

Organize a group to try some of the movement suggestions on these pages. Practice at school or at home.

DRESSING UP THE STEADY BEAT

Pretend to play steady beats on a bongo drum; your hands will make the same movements over and over.

Now vary your movement by playing the steady beat on imaginary drumheads that are placed in different parts of the room—ceiling, floor, door, opposite walls, and so forth. To do this without moving your feet, you will need to reach, stretch, and bend—high and low, forward and backward, and diagonally. Although the steady beat remains the same, your movement can have many variations.

Plan a phrase in which one movement moves into another. How long will your phrase of movement be? How will you begin? How will you end? After you have decided, ask someone to accompany your movement on a percussion instrument.

Experiment further by adding accents to your movements; by changing the tempo to very fast or very slow.

FANCY STEPPING TO THE STEADY BEAT

Keep time to the steady beat of *Shoeflies* by strutting on the first and third beats of each measure and adding a different movement on the second and fourth beats. You will find some suggestions for a fancy step at the right.

🔘 Sakayama: *Shoeflies*
10

Now plan a phrase of movement that combines two or more fancy steps.

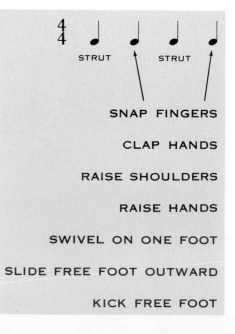

STRUT   STRUT

SNAP FINGERS

CLAP HANDS

RAISE SHOULDERS

RAISE HANDS

SWIVEL ON ONE FOOT

SLIDE FREE FOOT OUTWARD

KICK FREE FOOT

USING THE STEADY BEAT IN A LINE DANCE

After moving to the steady beat in *Shoeflies,* try this line dance with the same music. Find a place where you will have room to move backward, forward, and sideways.

PHRASE 1 (8 BEATS): WALK BACKWARD—RIGHT, LEFT, RIGHT. TOUCH FLOOR WITH LEFT FOOT.
WALK FORWARD—LEFT, RIGHT, LEFT. TOUCH FLOOR WITH RIGHT FOOT.

PHRASE 2 (8 BEATS): WALK SIDEWAYS AND STEP RIGHT, LEFT, RIGHT. TOUCH FLOOR WITH LEFT FOOT.
REPEAT TO THE LEFT—STEP LEFT, RIGHT, LEFT. TOUCH FLOOR WITH RIGHT FOOT.

PHRASE 3 (8 BEATS): STEP RIGHT, TOUCH LEFT NEXT TO RIGHT.
STEP LEFT, TOUCH RIGHT NEXT TO LEFT.
STEP RIGHT, TOUCH LEFT.
CLICK HEELS TWICE.

PHRASE 4 (8 BEATS): TAP FLOOR TWICE IN FRONT WITH RIGHT (2 BEATS).
TAP FLOOR TWICE IN BACK WITH RIGHT (2 BEATS).
TAP RIGHT FOOT ONCE FORWARD (1 BEAT), ONCE BACKWARD (1 BEAT), ONCE TO THE SIDE (1 BEAT).
PIVOT ON LEFT FOOT, MAKING A QUARTER TURN TO THE LEFT (1 BEAT). YOU ARE NOW FACING IN ANOTHER DIRECTION.

REPEAT FROM THE BEGINNING AS MANY TIMES AS DESIRED.

BLOCK-PASSING GAME

Sometimes the steady beat changes tempo. It gets faster or slower. How does the tempo change in the music for the block-passing game on page 6 in your book?

🔘 "Sasa Akroma"
1

Children in Brazil play a variation of this block-passing game with the song "Zigy, Zigy, Za" (page 58). The game is played exactly like Block-Passing Game, with one exception.

When you come to the words *zigy, zigy, za,* keep the block in your hand as you pretend to put it down and pick up another one. Continue passing the block on the word za.

 "Zigy, Zigy, Za"
3

SCHOTTISCHE: THE BEAT IN 4's

The basic step of the schottische is in $\frac{4}{4}$ meter. Before planning a group dance, try the basic step and the variation with the recording.

🔘
10 *Balkan Hills Schottische*

Basic Step

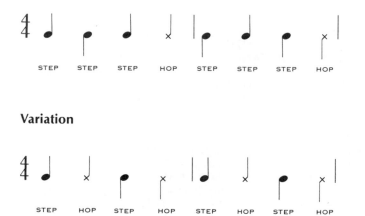

STEP   STEP   STEP   HOP   STEP   STEP   STEP   HOP

Variation

STEP   HOP   STEP   HOP   STEP   HOP   STEP   HOP

Now listen for the length of phrases in the music. Then try doing the basic step in different directions—forward, backward, diagonally, and around. Change direction for each new phrase.

SCHOTTISCHE DANCE

FORMATION:	PARTNERS STAND SIDE BY SIDE IN A CIRCLE, FACING COUNTERCLOCKWISE, AND WITH INSIDE HANDS JOINED.
PHRASE 1 (8 BEATS):	STARTING WITH OUTSIDE FOOT, TAKE TWO SCHOTTISCHE STEPS FORWARD.
PHRASE 2 (8 BEATS):	STARTING WITH OUTSIDE FOOT, TAKE TWO SCHOTTISCHE STEPS BACKWARD.
PHRASE 3 (8 BEATS):	TAKE ONE SCHOTTISCHE STEP SIDEWAYS, AWAY FROM YOUR PARTNER (4 BEATS). TAKE ONE SCHOTTISCHE STEP SIDEWAYS TOWARD YOUR PARTNER (4 BEATS).
PHRASE 4 (8 BEATS):	JOIN BOTH HANDS WITH YOUR PARTNER AND STEP-HOP (SCHOTTISCHE-STEP VARIATION) IN A CIRCLE IN PLACE, ENDING IN YOUR ORIGINAL POSITION, READY TO START THE DANCE AGAIN.

POLKA: THE BEAT IN 2's

Before trying the polka step, keep time to the rhythm of the polka music on the recording by galloping around the room.

🔟 *Emilia Polka*

Now try eight gallops with the right foot leading, followed by eight gallops with the left foot leading.

When you can change from right foot leading to left foot leading, try changing lead foot after every four gallops; after every two gallops. You are now doing the basic polka step, which has a feeling of a gallop.

Basic Step

$$\frac{2}{4} \quad \downarrow \quad \downarrow \quad | \downarrow. \quad \downarrow \downarrow | \downarrow \quad \downarrow \quad | \downarrow. \quad \downarrow |$$

STEP   TOGETHER.   STEP   HOP. STEP   TOGETHER.   STEP   HOP.

Try dancing the polka step to the music on the recording.

TWO VARIATIONS OF THE POLKA STEP

1. STAND SIDE BY SIDE WITH A PARTNER, INSIDE HANDS JOINED.

TOUCH R   TOUCH R   R   L   R   HOP TOUCH L   TOUCH L   L   R   L   HOP
HEEL TO   TOE TO   (POLKA STEP)   HEEL TO   TOE TO   (POLKA STEP)
FLOOR   FLOOR   FLOOR   FLOOR

2. FACING A PARTNER, WITH BOTH HANDS ON EACH OTHER'S SHOULDERS, SLIDE TO THE LEFT DURING ONE PHRASE (8 SLIDES). SLIDE TO THE RIGHT DURING THE NEXT PHRASE (8 SLIDES).

Make up your own dance by adding a phrase or more of each variation to the basic polka step.

Dayenu

HEBREW PASSOVER SONG   ENGLISH WORDS BY ELIZABETH S. BACHMAN   🔟

1. He has led us out of E - gypt, led His peo - ple out of E - gypt,

He has led us out of E - gypt, *da - ye - nu.*

REFRAIN

Da - da - ye - nu, _____ da - da - ye - nu, _____

Da - da - ye - nu, da - ye - nu da - ye - nu da - ye - nu,

Da - da - ye - nu, _____ da - da - ye - nu, _____

Da - da - ye - nu, da - ye - nu da - ye - nu.

2. He has given us the Sabbath, given us the holy Sabbath,
   He has given us the Sabbath, *dayenu. Refrain*

3. He has given us the Torah, given us the blessed Torah,
   He has given us the Torah, *dayenu. Refrain*

CIRCLE DANCE

Feel the beats in sets of four as you dance to the music of "Dayenu."

FORMATION: ANY NUMBER OF DANCERS STAND IN A CIRCLE (FACING THE CENTER) HOLDING JOINED HANDS AT SHOULDER LEVEL.

Section A (short phrases of 4 beats)

4 BEATS: STEP SIDEWAYS RIGHT, STEP LEFT IN BACK OF RIGHT, STEP RIGHT, STAMP LEFT.

4 BEATS: STEP SIDEWAYS LEFT, STEP RIGHT IN BACK OF LEFT, STEP LEFT, STAMP RIGHT.

4 BEATS: STEP FORWARD RIGHT, STAMP LEFT WHILE RAISING ARMS. STEP BACKWARD LEFT, STAMP RIGHT, LOWERING ARMS.

4 BEATS: STAMP RIGHT, LEFT, RIGHT, HOLD.

Section B (long phrases of 16 beats)

16 BEATS: WITH HANDS STILL JOINED, ALL TURN SLIGHTLY TO THE RIGHT AND DANCE 7 POLKA STEPS TO THE RIGHT, STARTING WITH RIGHT FOOT. (FOR BASIC POLKA STEP, SEE PAGE 241).
TO COMPLETE THE PHRASE, DROP HANDS, TURN AROUND TO THE RIGHT, AND QUICKLY JOIN HANDS AGAIN. THE CIRCLE IS NOW INSIDE OUT.

16 BEATS: DANCE 7 POLKA STEPS TO THE RIGHT, STARTING WITH THE RIGHT FOOT. TO COMPLETE THE PHRASE, DROP HANDS AND TURN RIGHT. THE CIRCLE IS NOW FACING CENTER AGAIN.

THE HORA

FORMATION: ANY NUMBER OF DANCERS STAND IN A CIRCLE, FACING TOWARD THE CENTER. EACH PERSON PLACES A HAND ON THE SHOULDER OF THE PERSON ON EACH SIDE.

1. STEP SIDEWAYS WITH LEFT FOOT.
2. STEP ON RIGHT FOOT, PLACING IT BEHIND LEFT FOOT.
3. STEP ON LEFT FOOT.
4. HOP ON LEFT FOOT, SWINGING RIGHT LEG IN FRONT.
5. STEP ON RIGHT FOOT.
6. HOP ON RIGHT FOOT, SWINGING LEFT LEG IN FRONT.
(REPEAT)

Practice the hora with the recording of one of the songs you know: "Tzena, Tzena," page 50; "Toembaï," page 10; "Zum Gali Gali," page 136.

GREEK DANCE

In this New Year's dance from Greece, the eight-step dance
pattern matches the length of each phrase in the music.
Directions for the eight-step dance pattern are written under
the first phrase of the music.

New Year Carol

(AS DANCED BY TULA LOMIS)   FOLK SONG FROM GREECE   ENGLISH WORDS BY STELLA PHREDOPOLOUS

Lift your voic - es, sing to - geth - er, wel - come the brand new year.

R = RIGHT FOOT STEP   CROSS L   STEP   CROSS L   STEP   POINT L   STEP POINT R
L = LEFT FOOT RIGHT   IN BACK   RIGHT   IN FRONT   RIGHT   IN FRONT   LEFT IN BACK
                       OF R   OF R

In this time of hap - pi - ness, this time of good cheer

Ban - ish all your cares, for on this ho - ly feast____

Saint Ba - sil comes bear - ing gifts of love and peace.

Practice the dance pattern until you can perform it in the
tempo of the music. Repeat the pattern throughout the dance.

OPEN CIRCLE DANCE

For a group dance, any number of dancers join hands in an
"open" circle and follow the leader.

GREEK DANCE IN 3's

Before trying the foot movements, listen for the tempo of the beat and play the rhythm of the basic pattern on a percussion instrument. The pattern uses half notes and quarter notes.

🔟 Traditional: *Tsamiko*

Basic Pattern

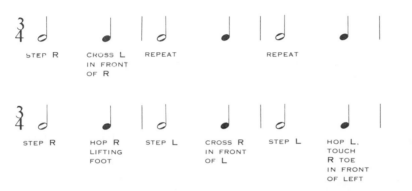

$\frac{3}{4}$

STEP R   CROSS L IN FRONT OF R   REPEAT   REPEAT

$\frac{3}{4}$

STEP R   HOP R LIFTING FOOT   STEP L   CROSS R IN FRONT OF L   STEP L   HOP L, TOUCH R TOE IN FRONT OF LEFT

Now do the foot pattern, following the basic rhythm pattern.

Try dancing in a group. With hands joined, form an open circle with a leader at one end. The leader, holding a handkerchief, moves the line about the room in snakelike fashion—weaving to the right, to the left, and so forth—while doing different tricks: leaping, dancing backward, and so on.

MEXICAN DANCE IN 3's

To feel the meter in 3, try this basic foot pattern. First practice it alone and then facing a partner.

Basic Pattern

When you can do the basic foot pattern, practice it with the music.

 "La Cucaracha"

Now, try doing a waltz-walk. Think "down, up, up."

Waltz-walk

DOWN	UP	UP	DOWN	UP	UP	DOWN	UP	UP
STEP L	R	L	R	L	R	L	R	L
WITH KNEE BENT	ON TIP-TOE	ON TIP-TOE						

LA CUCARACHA DANCE

When you can do the basic foot pattern and the waltz-walk, you are ready to use them in a dance.

FORMATION: ANY NUMBER OF PARTNERS, FACING EACH OTHER IN A SINGLE CIRCLE.

SECTION A: DANCE THE BASIC FOOT PATTERN.

SECTION B: PARTNERS STILL FACING, EACH DANCER WALTZ-WALKS FORWARD AROUND THE CIRCLE, PASSING RIGHT SHOULDERS.

AT THE END (CADENCE) OF SECTION B, DANCERS STOP IN FRONT OF A NEW PARTNER AND THE DANCE BEGINS AGAIN.

AN AMERICAN SQUARE DANCE

Camptown Races
STEPHEN FOSTER

SECTION A

Ladies to the center and go back home, Doodah, doodah,
(LADIES WALK FOUR STEPS FORWARD, TURN, WALK BACK TO ORIGINAL POSITION.)

Gents to the center with a right hand star, Oh, doodah day.
(GENTS WALK FORWARD WITH RIGHT HANDS OUTSTRETCHED, TOUCH HANDS IN THE CENTER AND MOVE CLOCKWISE ONCE AROUND THE CIRCLE TO ORIGINAL POSITIONS.)

Balance in and balance out, Doodah, doodah,
(JOIN LEFT HANDS WITH PARTNER AND RIGHT HANDS WITH CORNER. THE SQUARE BECOMES A CIRCLE WITH LADIES FACING IN AND GENTS FACING OUT. TAKE TWO STEPS FORWARD AND TWO STEPS BACK. DROP RIGHT HANDS. TURN PARTNER AROUND, KEEPING LEFT HANDS JOINED. JOIN RIGHT HANDS WITH NEW PARTNER.)

Turn with the left hand half about, Oh, doodah day.
(BALANCE IN AND BALANCE OUT. DROP LEFT HANDS WITH ORIGINAL PARTNER AND STAND SIDE BY SIDE WITH NEW PARTNER, READY TO PROMENADE.)

SECTION B

Refrain: Promenade
(WALK COUNTERCLOCKWISE AROUND THE CIRCLE AND BACK TO PLACE.)

AN EARLY AMERICAN DANCE ◉ *Cotton-Eyed Joe*
10

(As taught by Anne Simmons, University of Texas at Arlington)

FORMATION: A CIRCLE OF SETS OF TWO COUPLES—A LEAD COUPLE IN
FRONT OF A TRAILING COUPLE; INSIDE HANDS JOINED WITH
PARTNER AND OUTSIDE HANDS JOINED WITH THE PERSON IN
FRONT OR BEHIND. ALL FACE COUNTERCLOCKWISE.

Part I (4 measures)

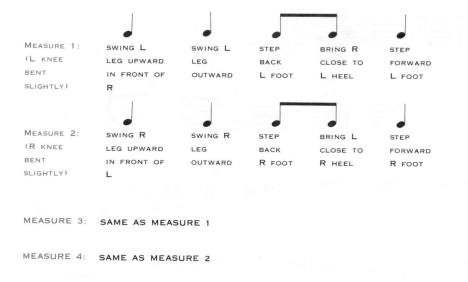

MEASURE 1:   SWING L   SWING L   STEP   BRING R   STEP
(L KNEE   LEG UPWARD   LEG   BACK   CLOSE TO   FORWARD
BENT   IN FRONT OF OUTWARD   L FOOT   L HEEL   L FOOT
SLIGHTLY)   R

MEASURE 2:   SWING R   SWING R   STEP   BRING L   STEP
(R KNEE   LEG UPWARD   LEG   BACK   CLOSE TO   FORWARD
BENT   IN FRONT OF OUTWARD   R FOOT   R HEEL   R FOOT
SLIGHTLY)   L

MEASURE 3:   SAME AS MEASURE 1

MEASURE 4:   SAME AS MEASURE 2

Part II (4 measures)

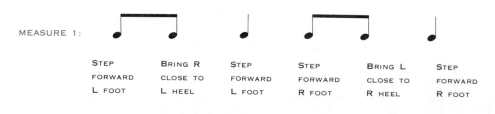

MEASURE 1:   STEP   BRING R   STEP   STEP   BRING L   STEP
FORWARD   CLOSE TO   FORWARD   FORWARD   CLOSE TO   FORWARD
L FOOT   L HEEL   L FOOT   R FOOT   R HEEL   R FOOT

MEASURES 2-4:   SAME AS MEASURE 1

THE TWO-STEP PATTERN IN PART II MOVES THE CIRCLE FORWARD COUNTERCLOCKWISE.

EACH PERSON IN THE LEAD COUPLE DROPS HANDS AND, TURNING LEFT OR RIGHT
(TOWARD THE OUTSIDE HAND), DANCES 8 TWO-STEPS AROUND AND BEHIND THE
TRAILING COUPLE. AT THE SAME TIME, THE TRAILING COUPLE, INSIDE HANDS STILL
JOINED. DANCES 8 TWO-STEPS FORWARD AND BECOMES THE NEW LEAD COUPLE.

PARTS I AND II MAY BE REPEATED OVER AND OVER TO THE END OF THE MUSIC.

THE COAL MINER'S SONG 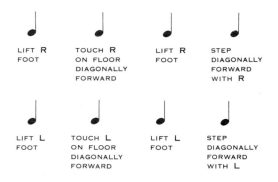 *Miike Tanko*

Work out each movement pattern described below. Then try doing the patterns with the recording.

Shoveling Coal (16 beats)

HOLDING AN IMAGINARY SHOVEL WITH BOTH HANDS, MAKE DIGGING MOTIONS. FOOT MOVEMENTS FOLLOW THE STEADY BEAT.

LIFT R FOOT   TOUCH R ON FLOOR DIAGONALLY FORWARD   LIFT R FOOT   STEP DIAGONALLY FORWARD WITH R

LIFT L FOOT   TOUCH L ON FLOOR DIAGONALLY FORWARD   LIFT L FOOT   STEP DIAGONALLY FORWARD WITH L

Carrying Coal (12 beats)

HOLD SHOVEL OVER R SHOULDER AND STEP FORWARD WITH R FOOT (2 BEATS). HOLD SHOVEL OVER L SHOULDER AND STEP FORWARD WITH L FOOT (2 BEATS). REPEAT R AND L SHOULDER PATTERNS TWO MORE TIMES.

Looking at the Moon (12 beats)

AS IF LOOKING AT THE MOON, STEP BACKWARD R, RAISING L ARM OVER HEAD AND HOLDING R ARM BEHIND WAIST (2 BEATS).

STEP BACKWARD L, RAISING R ARM AND HOLD L ARM BEHIND WAIST (2 BEATS).

REPEAT R AND L LOOKING-AT-THE-MOON PATTERNS TWO MORE TIMES.

Pushing the Coal Cart (12 beats)

LIFT R KNEE, THEN STEP FORWARD R, MAKING PUSHING MOTION WITH ARMS (2 BEATS).
LIFT L KNEE, THEN STEP FORWARD L, MAKING PUSHING MOTION WITH ARMS (2 BEATS).
REPEAT L AND R PUSHING PATTERN 2 MORE TIMES.

Ending Pattern (8 beats)

BENDING OVER SLIGHTLY FROM THE WAIST, START WITH HANDS CROSSED IN FRONT AND TRACE TWO LARGE CIRCLES BY MOVING EACH ARM OUTWARD TO THE SIDE, UP OVER THE HEAD, AND DOWN TO THE FRONT AGAIN (2 BEATS). CLAP HANDS THREE TIMES (YOI, YOI, YOI) AND GET READY TO BEGIN "SHOVELING COAL" AGAIN.

Sakura

AS DANCED BY SHERRY GEALY ⊙ 5

The movements for "Sakura," page 119, help to tell of the beauty of the cherry tree. Each movement is done first to the right and then to the left, filling one phrase of music.

Girls stand in any formation. For the beginning pose, rest right hand on top of left hand at waist level, with both palms up. After each pose in the dance, hands return to the beginning pose. Eyes should follow arm movements in each pose.

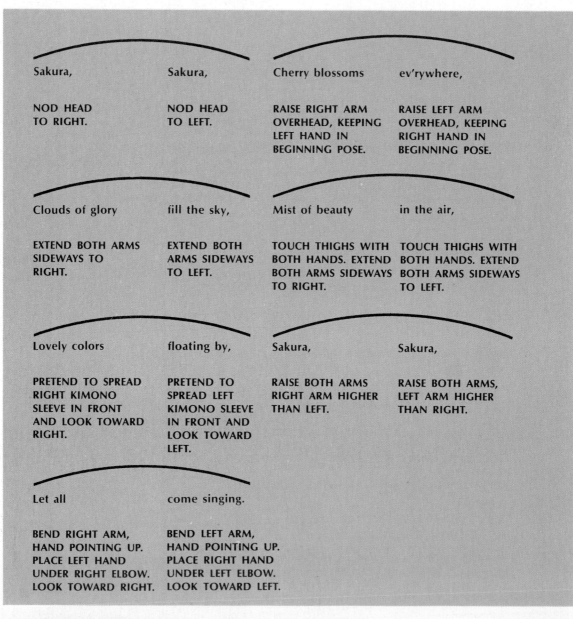

Sakura,   Sakura,   Cherry blossoms   ev'rywhere,

NOD HEAD
TO RIGHT.

NOD HEAD
TO LEFT.

RAISE RIGHT ARM
OVERHEAD, KEEPING
LEFT HAND IN
BEGINNING POSE.

RAISE LEFT ARM
OVERHEAD, KEEPING
RIGHT HAND IN
BEGINNING POSE.

Clouds of glory   fill the sky,   Mist of beauty   in the air,

EXTEND BOTH ARMS
SIDEWAYS TO
RIGHT.

EXTEND BOTH
ARMS SIDEWAYS
TO LEFT.

TOUCH THIGHS WITH
BOTH HANDS. EXTEND
BOTH ARMS SIDEWAYS
TO RIGHT.

TOUCH THIGHS WITH
BOTH HANDS. EXTEND
BOTH ARMS SIDEWAYS
TO LEFT.

Lovely colors   floating by,   Sakura,   Sakura,

PRETEND TO SPREAD
RIGHT KIMONO
SLEEVE IN FRONT
AND LOOK TOWARD
RIGHT.

PRETEND TO
SPREAD LEFT
KIMONO SLEEVE
IN FRONT AND
LOOK TOWARD
LEFT.

RAISE BOTH ARMS
RIGHT ARM HIGHER
THAN LEFT.

RAISE BOTH ARMS,
LEFT ARM HIGHER
THAN RIGHT.

Let all   come singing.

BEND RIGHT ARM,
HAND POINTING UP.
PLACE LEFT HAND
UNDER RIGHT ELBOW.
LOOK TOWARD RIGHT.

BEND LEFT ARM,
HAND POINTING UP.
PLACE RIGHT HAND
UNDER LEFT ELBOW.
LOOK TOWARD LEFT.

Songs that Tell Our Country's Story

Blow, Ye Winds

AMERICAN FOLK SONG

FROM SONGS OF AMERICAN SAILORMEN BY JOANNA C. COLCORD, BY PERMISSION OF
W. W. NORTON & COMPANY, INC. COPYRIGHT 1938 BY W. W. NORTON & COMPANY, INC. COPYRIGHT RENEWED 1966 BY THE BOONE COUNTY STATE BANK, LEBANON, INDIANA, EXECUTOR OF THE AUTHOR.

This song gives a picture of life in the days of the whaling ships that sailed out of New Bedford. Whaling crews signed on for a voyage that sometimes lasted for three years.

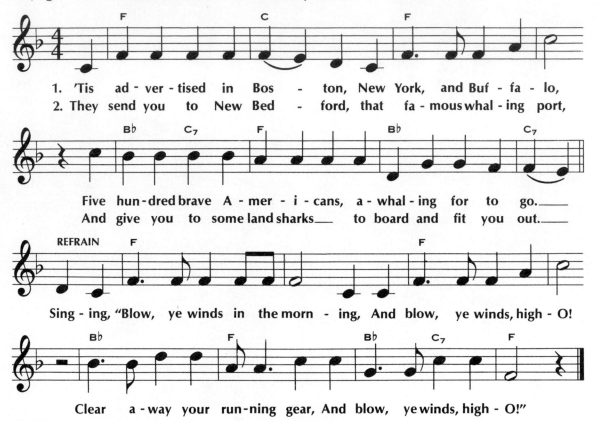

1. 'Tis ad-ver-tised in Bos-ton, New York, and Buf-fa-lo,
2. They send you to New Bed-ford, that fa-mous whal-ing port,

Five hun-dred brave A-mer-i-cans, a-whal-ing for to go.____
And give you to some land sharks____ to board and fit you out.____

REFRAIN

Sing-ing, "Blow, ye winds in the morn-ing, And blow, ye winds, high-O!

Clear a-way your run-ning gear, And blow, ye winds, high-O!"

3. They tell you of the clipper ships a-going in and out,
   And say you'll take five hundred sperm before you're six months out.

4. It's now we're out to sea, my boys, the wind begins to blow,
   One half the watch is sick on deck and the other half below.

5. The skipper's on the quarter-deck a-squinting at the sails,
   When up aloft the look-out sights a school of whales.

6. "Now clear away the boats, my boys, and after him we'll trail,
   But if you get too near to him, he'll kick you with his tail!"

7. Now we've got him turned up, we tow him alongside;
   We over with our blubber hooks and rob him of his hide.

8. Next comes the stowing down, my boys; 'twill take both night and day,
   And you'll all have fifty cents apiece when you collect your pay.

John Henry

FOLK SONG FROM SOUTHERN UNITED STATES

John Henry, a legendary character, was the southern
steel-driving man whose fame spread across the country. The
strength of his arm was greater than the power of a steam drill,
or so the story goes.

1. John___ Hen - ry___ told___ his cap - tain,
2. Well, the cap - tain___ says to John Hen - ry,

"Well, a man ain't noth - in' but a man,
"Gon - na bring that steam___ drill a - round,

But be - fore I let your drill___ beat me down,
Gon - na take that steam___ drill___ out on the job,

I'll___ die with a ham - mer in my hand."   hand."
Gon - na whop that___ steel___ on ___ down."   down."

3. Oh, the man that invented the steam drill,
   He thought that he was mighty fine,
   But John Henry drove his steel fifteen feet,
   And the steam drill drove only nine. (*2 times*)

4. John Henry was hammerin' on the mountain,
   There was lightnin' in his eye.
   He drove so hard that he broke his heart,
   And he laid down his hammer and he died. (*2 times*)

Erie Canal

AMERICAN FOLK SONG

PUBLISHED BY PERMISSION OF THE COPYRIGHT OWNER, JERRY VOGEL MUSIC CO., INC.

The Erie Canal was once a busy waterway between Albany and Buffalo. The boats were pulled along by mules or horses, which walked on the towpath at the side of the canal.

SOLO   D MIN.   G MIN.   A₇

1. I got a___ mule, her name is___ Sal,
2. Git up there,___ Sal, we passed that___ lock,

CHORUS
D MIN.

Fif - teen___ miles on the E - rie Ca - nal!

SOLO
D MIN.   G MIN.   A₇

She's a good old___ work - er and a good old___ pal,
And___ we'll make___ Rome___ 'fore___ six o' - clock,

CHORUS
D MIN.

Fif - teen___ miles on the E - rie Ca - nal!

SOLO   F   A₇

We've hauled some barg - es in our___ day,
Just one more trip and back we'll___ go

Filled with lum - ber, coal, and_____ hay,
Through the rain and sleet and_____ snow,

And we know ev - 'ry inch of the way
'Cause we know ev - 'ry inch of the way

From Al - ba - ny_____ to_____ Buf - fa - lo.

REFRAIN
CHORUS

Low bridge, ev - 'ry - bod - y down,

Low bridge, 'cause we're com - ing to a town;

And you'll al - ways know your neigh-bor, You'll al - ways know your pal,

If you ev - er nav - i - gat - ed on the E - rie Ca - nal._____

Wabash Cannon Ball

TRADITIONAL

During the 1800s, railroads spread in a huge network across the country. This rollicking song tells about the wonders of a train called the *Wabash Cannon Ball.*

1. From the rock - y bound At - lan - tic   to the blue Pa - cif - ic
   name of mag - ic splen - dor   that is known quite well to

shore,   From the warm and sun - ny South - land   to the
all,   'Tis the won - drous com - bi - na - tion   called the

isle of La - bra - dor,   There's a *Wa - bash Can - non   Ball.*

REFRAIN

Then lis - ten to the jin - gle,   the rum - ble, and the roar   of the

might - y rush - ing en - gine   as she streams a - long the shore,   Hear the

thun - der on the steel rails,   hear the bell and whis - tle call,   As you

roll a - long in safe - ty   on the *Wa - bash Can - non   Ball.*

256

2. Great cities of importance are reached along its way,
    Chicago and Saint Louis, and Rock Island, so they say,
    And Springfield and Decatur, and Peoria, last of all
    'Tis the western termination of the *Wabash Cannon Ball.*
    Refrain

You will find the names of six cities in the words of verse 2 of
"Wabash Cannon Ball." Call out the names as an introduction
to the song.

Shoot the Buffalo   PLAY-PARTY SONG FROM OKLAHOMA

People worked hard to build our country. But they took time
for entertainment, too. This play-party song was used at
gatherings all over the South and the West.

1. Rise you up, my dear-est dear, and pre-sent to me your hand,
2. Where the la-dies knit and sew, and the gents they plow and hoe,

We are roam-ing in suc-ces-sion to some far and dis-tant land,
Then we'll ram-ble in the cane-brake, and we'll shoot the buf-fa-lo.

To some far and dis-tant land, to some far and dis-tant land,
And we'll shoot the buf-fa-lo, and we'll shoot the buf-fa-lo,

We are roam-ing in suc-ces-sion to some far and dis-tant land.
Then we'll ram-ble in the cane-brake, and we'll shoot the buf-fa-lo.

Sweet Betsy from Pike

AMERICAN FOLK SONG

The hardy pioneers of our country rolled over the western trails in covered wagons. Songs like this one kept their spirits high and helped them to laugh at their hardships.

1. Oh, don't you re - mem - ber sweet Bet - sy from Pike?
2. One ev' - ning quite ear - ly they camped on the Platte,

She crossed the broad prai - ries with her hus - band, Ike,
'Twas near by the road on a green shad - y flat.

With two yoke of ox - en, an old yel - low dog,
Poor Bet - sy, quite tired,_____ lay down for re - pose,

A_____ tall Shang - hai roost - er and one spot - ted hog.
And_____ Ike sat and gazed at his Pike Coun - ty rose.

REFRAIN

Too - ra - lay,_____ too - ra - lay,

Sing - ing too - ra - li, too - ra - li, too - ra - li - ay.

3. They soon reached the desert where Betsy gave out,
   And down on the sand she lay rolling about.
   While Ike, in great tears, looked on in surprise:
   Said, "Betsy, get up, you'll get sand in your eyes." *Refrain*

258

4. The rooster ran off and the oxen all died;
   The last piece of bacon that morning was fried.
   Poor Ike got discouraged and Betsy got mad;
   The dog wagged his tail and looked awfully sad. *Refrain*

5. The alkali desert was burning and hot,
   And Ike, he decided to leave on the spot:
   "My dear old Pike County, I'll go back to you."
   Said Betsy, "You'll go by yourself if you do." *Refrain*

6. They swam the wide rivers, they crossed the tall peaks,
   They camped out on prairies for weeks and for weeks,
   Fought hunger and rattlers and big storms of dust,
   Determined to reach California or bust. *Refrain*

Colorado Trail   AMERICAN FOLK SONG

This song expresses the loneliness often felt by the cowboys
during the long night watches on the Colorado Trail.

Eyes like a morn-ing star, Cheeks like a rose,

Lau-ra was a pret-ty girl, Ev-'ry-bod-y knows.

Weep, all ye lit-tle rains, Wail, winds,____ wail,

All a-long, a-long, a-long the Col-o-ra-do Trail.

Dogie Song

AMERICAN COWBOY SONG

Cowboys sang as they rode on the western plains. They used their songs to keep the cattle moving during the day and to quiet them at night.

In this song, the horse lopes along gently while the cowboy encourages the dogies (motherless calves) to keep pace with the herd.

1. As I was a - walk - ing one morn - ing for pleas - ure,
2. It's whoop - ing and yell - ing and driv - ing the do - gies,

I spied a cow - punch - er a - rid - ing a - long;
And oh, how I wish you would on - ly go on:

His hat was thrown back and his spurs were a - jin - gling,
It's whoop - ing and punch - ing, go on, lit - tle do - gies,

And as he ap - proached he was sing - ing this song:
You know that Wy - o - ming will be your new home.

REFRAIN

Whoop - ee - ti - yi - yo,____ git a - long, lit - tle do - gies,

It's your mis - for - tune and none of my own.

Whoop-ee - ti - yi - yo,_____ git a - long, lit - tle do - gies,

You know that Wy - o - ming will be your new home.

3. Some boys they go up the trail just for pleasure,
   But that's where they get it awfully wrong;
   For nobody knows all the trouble they give us
   While we go driving them all along.

ADD A COUNTERMELODY

Here is a countermelody for voices, bells, or recorder.

REFRAIN

Whoop-ee - ti - yi - yo,_____   Whoop-ee - ti - yi - yo,_____

Whoop-ee - ti - yi - yo,_____   Whoop-ee - ti - yi - yo, Whoop-ee - ti - yi - yo.

The Owl (El Tecolote)

SPANISH-AMERICAN FOLK SONG

12

Many early settlers in the American Southwest were Spanish-speaking people. Some of their songs and stories told of *El Tecolote,* the little owl.

1. Te - co - lo - te, where do you come from? Te - co - lo - te, where do you come from?
come to bring you a warn - ing, I have come to bring you a warn - ing,

From Pueb - lo in Col - or - a - do, From Pueb - lo in Col - or - a - do,
That your love has gone __ and left you, That your love has gone __ and left you,

cu. _____
cu. _____

1.   2.   REFRAIN
                              I have   Lit - tle bird

cu, __ cu, __ cu, Lit - tle bird cu, __ cu, __ cu; Poor lit - tle

owl - et, an - i - mal - i - to, So, so hun - gry, te - co - lo - ti - to, cu. _____

2. Little owl, so brave and valiant,
   Little owl, so brave and valiant,
   How you sing in January,
   How you sing in January, cu.
   Why don't you all get together,
   Why don't you all get together
   And make a *tecolotero,*
   And make a *tecolotero,* cu?
   Refrain

Here are the Spanish words for the song. Try to follow them as you listen to the recording. You might want to try singing along.

1. *¿Tecolote, de donde vienes?*
   ¿Tecolote, de donde vienes?
   De Pueblo de Colorado,
   De Pueblo de Colorado, cu.
   Vengo a traerte la noticia,
   Vengo a traerte la noticia,
   Que tu amor está perdido,
   Que tu amor está perdido, cu.
   Refrain
   Pajaro cu, cu, cu,
   Pajaro cu, cu, cu;
   Probrecito animalito,
   Tiene hambre el tecolotito, cu.

2. *Tecolotito valiente,*
   Tecolotito valiente,
   Que cantastes en enero,
   Que cantastes en enero, cu.
   ¿Porque no se juntan todos,
   Porque no se juntan todos
   Y hacen un tecolotero,
   Y hacen un tecolotero, cu?
   Refrain
   Pajaro cu, cu, cu,
   Pajaro cu, cu, cu;
   Probrecito animalito,
   Tiene hambre el tecolotito, cu.

Play the maracas during the refrain.

Maracas

Laredo

MEXICAN FOLK SONG   ENGLISH WORDS BY MARGARET MARKS

The Spanish guitar is a popular instrument in Mexico. Use an
Autoharp to accompany this folk song. It will sound a little like
a Spanish guitar.

1. I'm off for Laredo, farewell, my love, I'm sorry to cause you pain; Don't follow across the prairie, my love, Don't follow me where I go.

I promise to send a letter, my love, To say when we'll meet again. But wait till I send a message, my love, Till then I will miss you so.

2. I've brought you a hand-sewn saddle, my love,
A blanket and bridle fine,
So when you go past the bunkhouse, my love,
The cowboys will know you're mine.
I've brought you a key of silver, my love,
Attached by a golden chain,
To lock up your heart forever, my love,
If never we meet again.

Captain Jinks

AMERICAN SQUARE DANCE TUNE

1. I'm___ Cap - tain Jinks of the Horse Ma - rines; I feed my horse
2. I___ joined my corps___ when twent - y - one, Of course I thought

on corn and beans, And court young la - dies in their teens,
it cap-i - tal fun; When the ene - my came, then off I'd run,

Though a cap - tain in the Ar - my. I teach young la - dies
For I wasn't cut out for the Ar - my. When I left home, Ma -

how to dance, How to dance, how to dance, I teach young la - dies
ma, she cried, Ma-ma, she cried, Ma-ma, she cried. When I left home, Ma -

how to dance, For I'm the pet of the Ar - my.
ma she cried, "He's not cut out for the Ar - my!"

REFRAIN

I'm___ Cap - tain Jinks of the Horse Ma - rines;

I feed my horse on corn and beans, And of - ten live

be - yond the means Of a Cap - tain in the Ar - my.

You're a Grand Old Flag

WORDS AND MUSIC BY GEORGE M. COHAN

Make up a drum part to play with this song.

You're a grand old flag, you're a high-fly-ing flag;

And for-ev-er in peace may you wave;

You're the em-blem of the land I love,

The home of the free and the brave.

Ev-ery heart beats true un-der red, white, and blue,

Where there's nev-er a boast or brag;

But should auld ac-quaint-ance be for-got,

Keep your eye on the grand old flag.

Glossary

absolute music   Music that has no suggestion of any nonmusical thing, idea, story, or event (*see* program music).

accent   A single tone or chord louder than those around it.

accompaniment   Music that supports the sound of a solo performer.

atonal   Music in which no single tone is a "home base" or "resting place."

ballad   In music, a song that tells a story.

beat   A repeating pulse that can·be felt in some music.

cadence   A group of chords or notes at the end of a phrase or piece that gives a feeling of pausing or finishing.

call and response   A musical device with a portion of a melody (call) followed by an answering portion (response). The response may imitate the call or it may be a separate melody that repeats each time.

canon   A device in which a melody begins in one part, and then is imitated by other parts in an overlapping fashion (*see* round).

chant   To sing in a manner approximating speech.

chord   Three or more different tones played or sung together.

chord pattern   An arrangement of chords into a small grouping, usually occurring often in a piece.

chorus   (*See* refrain.)

clef   A sign that tells where pitches are located on the staff. The sign 𝄞 (G clef, or treble clef) shows that G above middle C is on the second line. This clef is used for music in higher registers. The sign 𝄢 (F clef, or bass clef) shows the tone F below middle C on the fourth line. It is used for music in lower registers.

cluster   A group of tones very close together performed at the same time; used mostly in modern music.

composer   A person who makes up pieces of music by putting sounds together in his or her own way.

contour   The "shape" of a melody, made by the way it moves upward and downward in steps and leaps, and by repeated tones.

contrast   Two or more things that are different. In music, slow is a *contrast* to fast; section A is a *contrast* to section B.

countermelody   A melody that is played or sung at the same time as the main melody.

density   The thickness or thinness of sound.

duration   The length of sounds, from very short to very long.

dynamics   The loudness and softness of sounds.

elements   The parts out of which whole works of art are made: for example, music uses the *elements* melody, rhythm, texture, tone color, form; painting uses line, color, space, shape, etc.

ensemble   A group of players or singers.

fermata   A sign (⌢) indicating that a note is held longer than its written note value, stopping or "holding" the beat.

frets   Strips of metal across the fingerboard of guitars and similar instruments. The player raises the pitch of a string by pressing it into contact with a fret.

form   The overall plan of a piece of music.

fugue   A musical procedure based on imitation, in which the main melody (subject) and related melodies are repeated in higher and lower registers and in different keys. The texture is polyphonic.

ground   A melody pattern repeated over and over in the bass (lowest part) of a piece, while other things happen above it.

harmony   Two or more tones sounding at the same time.

improvisation   Making up music as it is being performed; often used in jazz.

interval   The distance between tones. The smallest interval in traditional Western music is the half-step (f–f$^\sharp$, f$^\sharp$–g, etc.), but contemporary music and music of other cultures often use smaller intervals.

jazz   A style that grew out of the music of black Americans, then took many different substyles— ragtime, blues, cool jazz, swing, bebop, rock, etc.

key   The particular scale on which a piece of music or section is based, named for its tonic, or key-tone, or "home-base" tone. (The key of D major indicates that the major scale starting and ending on the tone D is being used. *See* tonality.)

major scale   An arrangement of eight tones in a scale according to the following intervals, or steps: whole, whole, half, whole, whole, whole, half.

267

measure A grouping of beats set off by bar lines.

melody A line of single tones that move upward, downward, or repeat.

melody pattern An arrangement of pitches into a small grouping, usually occurring often in a piece.

meter The way the beats of music are grouped, often in sets of two or in sets of three. The meter signature, or time signature, such as $\frac{3}{4}$ or $\frac{4}{4}$, tells how many beats are in the group, or measure (top number), and the kind of note that gets one beat (bottom number).

minor scale Several arrangements of eight tones in a scale, such as *natural minor* (whole, half, whole, whole, half, whole, whole) and *melodic minor* (upward: whole, half, whole, whole, whole, whole, half; downward: whole, whole, half, whole, whole, half, whole).

notes Symbols for sound in music.

octave The distance of eight steps from one tone to another that has the same letter name. On the staff these steps are shown by the lines and spaces. When notes are an *octave* apart, there are eight lines and spaces from one note to the other.

ornamentation In the arts, the addition of decorations, or embellishments, to the basic structure of the work.

ostinato A rhythmic or melodic phrase that keeps repeating throughout a piece or a section of a piece.

pattern In the arts, an arrangement of an element or elements into a grouping, usually occurring often in the work (*see* elements).

phrase A musical sentence. Each *phrase* expresses one thought. Music is made up of *phrases* that follow one another in a way that sounds right.

pitch The highness or lowness of a tone.

polyrhythm Several different rhythm patterns going on at the same time, often causing conflicts of meter among them.

program music Music that suggests or describes some nonmusical idea, story, or event (*see* absolute music).

range In a melody, the span from the lowest tone to the highest tone.

refrain A part of a song that repeats, with the same music and words. It is often called the "chorus," since it is usually sung by all the singers, while the verses in between are often sung by one voice.

register The pitch location of a group of tones (*see* pitch). If the group of tones are all high sounds, they are in a high *register*. If the group of tones are all low sounds, they are in a low *register*.

repetition Music that is the same, or almost the same, as music that was heard earlier.

rests Symbols for silences in music.

rhythm The way movement is organized in a piece of music, using beat, no beat, long and short sounds, meter, accents, no accents, tempo, syncopation, etc.

rhythm pattern A pattern of long and short sounds.

rondo A musical form in which a section is repeated, with contrasting sections in between (such as A B A C A).

round A kind of canon that leads back to the beginning of the melody and starts all over again (circle canon).

scale An arrangement of pitches from lower to higher according to a specific pattern of intervals. Major, minor, pentatonic, whole-tone, and chromatic are five kinds of scales. Each one has its own arrangement of pitches.

sequence The repetition of a melody pattern at a higher or lower pitch level.

solo Music for a single player or singer, often with an accompaniment.

staff A set of five horizontal lines on which music notes are written.

style The overall effect a work of art makes by the way its elements are used (*see* elements). When works of art use elements similarly, they are said to be "in the same style."

subject *See* fugue.

syncopation An arrangement of rhythm in which prominent or important tones begin on weak beats or weak parts of beats, giving a catchy, off-balance movement to the music.

tempo The speed of the beat in a piece of music (*see* beat).

texture The way melody and harmony go together: a melody alone, two or more melodies together, or a melody with chords.

theme An important melody that occurs several times in a piece of music.

tonal Music that focuses on one tone that is more important than the others—a "home base"—or resting tone.

tonality The kind of scale, major or minor, on which a piece of music or section is based (*see* key).

tone color The special sound that makes one instrument or voice sound different from another.

tone row An arrangement of the twelve tones of the chromatic scale into a series in which there is no focus on any one of them as the home tone. When the series is played backward, it is called the "retrograde."

triplet A rhythm pattern made by dividing a beat into three equal sounds.

variation Music that is repeated but changed in some important way.

Index

Acknowledgments

Credit and appreciation are due publishers and copyright owners for use of the following.

"City" from GOLDEN SLIPPERS by Langston Hughes. Copyright © 1958 by Langston Hughes. Reprinted by permission of Harold Ober Associates, Inc.

"Fourth of July Night" from COMPLETE POEMS by Carl Sandburg. Copyright 1950 by Carl Sandburg. Reprinted by permission of Harcourt Brace Jovanovich, Inc.

"Summer Grass" from GOOD MORNING, AMERICA, copyright 1928, 1956 by Carl Sandburg. Reprinted by permission of Harcourt Brace Jovanovich, Inc.

"Swift Things Are Beautiful" reprinted with permission of The Macmillan Company from AWAY GOES SALLY by Elizabeth J. Coatsworth. Copyright 1934 by The Macmillan Company, renewed 1962 by Elizabeth Coatsworth Beston.

Picture Credits

Cover: Silver Burdett

2: t. Silver Burdett photo. 3.: E. Simonsen from Shostal Associates. 5: t. Silver Burdett photograph; b. Victoria Beller-Smith for Silver Burdett. 7: Silver Burdett photograph. 13: W. Bryant from Camera 5. 17: Silver Burdett photograph. 19: Victoria Beller-Smith for Silver Burdett. 29. Leon Kofod. 30: t., b.l. William M. Anderson; m. Silver Burdett photograph; b.r. Lee Lyon from Bruce Coleman, Inc. 34: l. Al Freni; t.r. © Paolo Koch from Photo Researchers, Inc.; b.r. © Gerry Granham from Photo Researchers, Inc. 38-9: Aron & Falcone, Inc. 40: Victoria Beller-Smith for Silver Burdett. 42: t.l. Stumbaugh from Taurus Photos, t.r. Steve Scheerer from Taurus Photos; b. Baron Wolman from Woodfin Camp & Associates, Inc. 43: t.l. C. B. Jones from Taurus; t.r. Clyde Smith from Peter Arnold. 73: Ken Regan from Camera 5. 78: t. Hiroji Kubota form Magnum; b. Victoria Beller-Smith for Silver Burdett. 79: t.l, t.r Victoria Beller-Smith for Silver Burdett; m.r. Ursula Kreis from DPI; b.r. Harald Sund. 81: Victoria Beller-Smith for Silver Burdett. 82: Silver Burdett photograph. 83: t., 1. & m.r. Yoram Kahana from Peter Arnold; b.r. Richard Weiss from Peter Arnold. 85–94: Silver Burdett photograph. 97: Aron & Falcone, Inc. 98: Silver Burdett photographs. 100: t.l. no credit; b. & r. Victoria Beller-Smith for Silver Burdett. 101: t.l. no credit; t.r. Mahon from Monkmeyer Press Photo Service; b. Victoria Beller-Smith for Silver Burdett. 103: Wright from Taurus Photos. 104: Silver Burdett photographs. 105: no credit. 106: Victoria Beller-Smith for Silver Burdett. 107: Silver Burdett photograph. 109: National Audubon Society from Photo Researchers, Inc. 110: t. Silver Burdett photograph; b. Robert Phillips from Peter Arnold. 111: t. Silver Burdett photograph; b. Frank Chesek from Aron & Falcone, Inc. 113: t. Pierre Wolff from Photo Researchers, Inc.; b. Van Bucher from Photo Researchers, Inc. 116: William M. Anderson. 119: C. Wilfong from Leo DeWys, Inc. 121: Arthur Tress from Magnum. 122 & 123: Terry Eiler. 124: John W. Cook. 130: The Bettmann Archive, Inc. 131: Elliot Landy from Magnum. 146–7: Victoria Beller-Smith from Silver Burdett. 164: Aron & Falcone, Inc. 166: Michael Alexander from Black Star. 168: Marc Riboud from Magnum. 170: b.l. Victoria Beller-Smith for Silver Burdett; m. Courtesy, C.B.S. Television; b.r. Peter Simons from DPI; t.l. Jules Zalon from DPI. 171: t.r. Fred Fehl; b. Jerome Kresch from Peter Arnold. 172: Silver Burdett photograph. 189–202: Victoria Beller-Smith for Silver Burdett. 205–217: Silver Burdett photographs. 221 & 237: Victoria Beller-Smith for Silver Burdett. 245: Silver Burdett photograph. 251: t. Matt Greene; b. Victoria Beller-Smith for Silver Burdett.

3 4 5 6 7 8 9 10—RRD—88 87 86 85

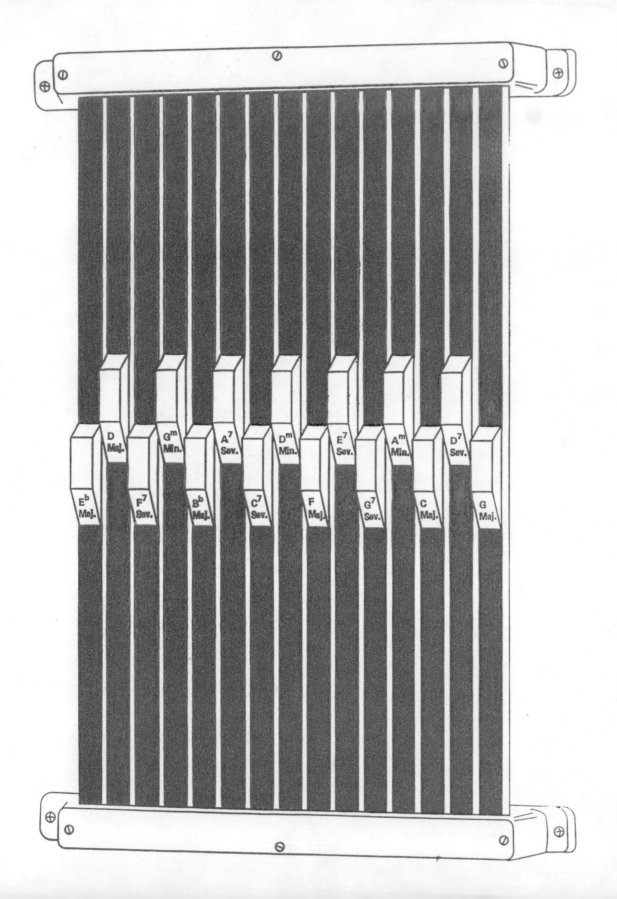